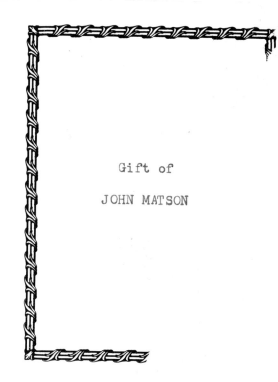

THE LIFE STORY OF
MARY STEVENSON, AUTHOR OF
THE IMMORTAL POEM

Footprints

IN THE SAND

gail giorgio

GOLD LEAF PRESS

Footprints in the Sand
The Life Story of Mary Stevenson, Author of the
Immortal Poem

Copyright © 1995 by Gail Giorgio
All rights reserved.

Library of Congress Cataloging-in-Publication Data

Brewer-Giorgio, Gail.
Footprints in the Sand: the inspiring life behind the
immortal poem/ by Gail Giorgio.
            p.   cm.
    1. Stevenson, Mary, 1922- Footprints in the Sand. 2.
Women poets, American—20th century—Biography.
3. Christian poetry—Authorship.   I. Title.
PS3569. T4563F66   1995
811'.54—DC20
[B]   95-1149
                                             CIP

ISBN 1-882723-12-0 (Paperback)
ISBN 1-882723-24-4 (Hardcover)

Printed in the United States of America

10   9   8   7   6   5   4   3   2

Art Direction: Richard Erickson
Cover Design: Ron Stucki
Cover Photo: © Douglas Pulsipher

Footprints

······································

IN THE SAND

DEDICATION

WITH MUCH LOVE AND gratitude, this book is dedicated to my beloved late husband, Basil Zangare, who always had faith in me, who always believed that the story behind the writing of "Footprints in the Sand" would eventually be told.

To that late, great entertainer Ethel Waters, who has found her "Cabin in the Sky," I'd like to say that the "White Cracker" is still dancing.

I thank God for sending into my life the Beautiful People: Chief War Bonnet, Corrine Woodfork, Paul Duggin, Mitch Pogue, Kathy Bee, Don Hampton, and especially Gail Giorgio—who in order to understand took the time to "walk a mile in my moccasins."

Mary Stevenson

I do not believe in coincidences, but rather believe that the souls of those we meet are drawn to us for a reason. Sometimes we're too busy with our everyday lives to notice the many interventions that God energizes.

God has blessed this world with his Special Angels, one being Mary Stevenson.

Many spiritual hugs and "light" to my husband, Carm; Mom and Dad Giorgio; children: Jim, Chris, and Maria, and their families; to attorney Tom Austin; to Candi Long, Vena Seibert, Erv Melton, and Kathy and Don Hampton (my cheerleaders!). To Gold Leaf's Mitch Pogue, Darla Isackson, Giles Florence, Jennifer Utley, Paul Rawlins, Richard Erickson, Janet Bernice, and Rebecca Porter. Thanks!

And always to my "Aunt Mim" and "Uncle Lee" whose "Footprints" have carried so many of us through difficult times!

We met this time—and we shall meet again.

Gail Giorgio

TABLE OF CONTENTS

FOREWORD

In 1990 the TV show A Current Affair featured an interview with Kimberly Bergalis, the young girl who had contracted AIDS from her dentist. She and the interviewer were walking along a beach in Florida. Already thin and weak, Kimberly was asked what kept her going. With a brave smile on her face, she quietly said, "Footprints in the Sand."

Kimberly died on December 8, 1991. But before she passed over to the other side, she knew beyond a shadow of a doubt that, "The years when you have seen only one set of footprints, my child, is when I carried you."

I CANNOT RECALL EXACTLY when I first read "Footprints in the Sand." I believe it was on a greeting card. It had to be prior to 1958 because that year I listed it in "My Secret Self Diary" which is stored in a box of high school memorabilia.

I knew that the creator of "Footprints in the Sand" was listed as "Author Unknown." I also knew that the most electrifying poem of this century had not written itself.

When Mary Stevenson, a descendant of Robert Louis Stevenson, contacted me and asked me to help her tell her story, I found myself deeply moved. She still had in her possession that crumpled yellow piece of paper where over fifty years ago she penned the words that would forever inspire both pauper and king.

As I began going through the weathered boxes containing the written remnants of Mary's walk through life, as I read and reread the more than 4,000 poems that she had penned since "Footprints," I thought how ironic it was that her own life was such a parallel to the poem she had written as a child.

Although she has received many accolades over the years for numerous good deeds, personal recognition for her greatest creation, "Footprints in the Sand," has passed her by.

Until now.

The story behind the writing of "Footprints in the Sand" is not only Mary's story, but yours and mine . . .

Gail Giorgio

Prologue

HER RIGHT HAND TREMBLED as she reached up toward the delicately framed poem hanging on the wall of a gift store. Even after all these years the sight of the words—now encased in tinted glass—made her breath catch. As her eyes filled with tears, a flash of memories became a kaleidoscope of colors in her mind.

The poem was surrounded by delicate leaves of gold intermingled with tiny pink roses. As she read the words, more familiar to her than to anyone else on earth, her memories seemed too many to visit in one lifetime.

Somehow she had been given so many truths in her poetry. In a small way she had removed some of the mystery of God and revealed Him.

Her pulse quickened and her eyes turned sad when—after rereading the poem that she had written as a child—she read the familiar:

"Author Unknown"

Mary became the "White Cracker" when, at the age of three, she began dancing for pennies with black children on the street corner.

Ethel Waters, who was Mary's neighbor and a frequent participant in neighborhood song and dance fests. (circa 1935)

Mary, baby Andy, and Tony on a rare family outing. Mary was separated from Tony at the time this picture was taken. (circa 1943)

Mary, after she was working as a nurse's aide in Methodist Hospital. On the back of the picture she wrote: "First purse and halfway decent clothes I bought—even lipstick!" (circa 1950)

Mary as "Stevie Richards" during the time she was dancing at the Troc burlesque house. (circa 1943)

Mary with the love of her
life, her second husband,
Basil. (circa 1950)

Mary and her second son,
Basil, Jr. (circa 1956)

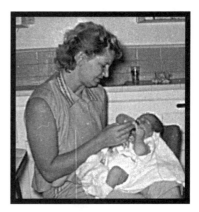

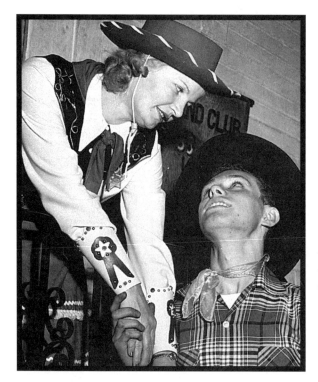

Mary as a lead in the play *Meet Arizona.*

Mary working at Katella Hospital after Basil's accident. (1950s)

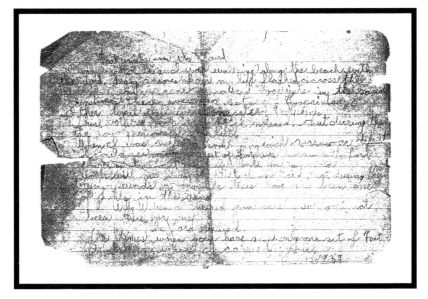

Handwritten copy of Mary's "Footprints" poem which she carried with her for years. This copy is dated 1939.

Angel with a Broken Wing

"Likely as not, the child you can do the least with will do the most to make you proud."
—Mignon McLaughlin

KNEELING ON THE WORN couch and staring through the snow-brushed window of her small row house, six-year-old Mary Stevenson saw her mother's face through a vapor of tears. Mary wiped her eyes on the shoulder of her cotton nightgown. Then her dimpled mouth trembled as her large, soft eyes filled once again.

For miles in every direction, the city was being blanketed by a sudden snowstorm, which left the normally brutal landscape buried in a quiet and unreal serenity. The cement jungle, now covered by a white canopy, appeared as a wilderness, a land untouched by human motion, or human footprints. The only sound was Mary's muted sobbing.

Even though the windowpane was cold, Mary's face remained warm with the blush of morning and with a sorrow that could not leave. As she had done every day since her mother had died, she asked the same question: What was "death," really? She stared blankly, then squinted, searching for an imperceptible answer. Death, the dreadful explanation to her mother's absence, was as mysterious as the terror she had felt while at the cemetery. She would never, ever, go to a cemetery again!

When a voice from behind her called her name, Mary winced. She turned and stared angrily at her father, not knowing why she wanted to blame him for her mother's leaving. All she knew was that it felt good to blame someone. There had been times when she blamed her mother. Before leaving for the sanitarium, her mother had given Mary a Kewpie doll on a cane. Although the doll wore an impish expression, the pink feathers on its back made it look like an angel. They had admired it together, then her mother had said, "You be a good little girl, Stevie. Help your daddy by looking after Dottie."

"When will you be back?" she had pleaded.

"Soon," her mother had promised. "Soon. . ."

But she didn't return soon. Instead she wrote Mary from the hospital. Then, a few hours after Mary had received the card from her mother saying that she was doing fine, a telegram arrived stating that her mother had died. Seeing her mother lying cold and lifeless in the open coffin did little to ease the heartache of a "broken promise."

Mary also blamed her brothers and sisters for her mother's absence and often took it upon herself to remind them of every deed they had ever done that might have caused their mother distress. She was careful to eliminate from her thoughts anything that she might have done. She preferred her own image to remain as pure and stain-free as the virgin snow falling outside her window. It was as if she were confirming her own belief that her mother had loved her best—a distorted idea, but one which she thought possible.

"Stevie," her father said gently, "it's time for you to get ready for school."

Unable to stand the misery and despair in her father's eyes, Mary turned back to the window.

"Daddy? I think you should cover Mom with a blanket. It's snowing. She'll get cold in the ground."

Andrew Stevenson felt his breath catch as he stood quietly until his sudden nausea subsided. The thought of Louise in the hard, ice-covered earth seemed too impossible to grasp. Her presence still filled the house as her lingering scent floated from room to room.

It had been impossible to sleep in their bed, or touch the pillow where Louise had placed her head.

Drawing up straight, Andrew sighed. He must close the door to the memory of Louise; he must accept the fact that never again would she wake up at his side. "The dead don't feel cold or pain, child," he finally answered. "Pain is only for the living."

The coldness in her father's voice confirmed what Mary had imagined: her father had not loved her mother as she had, and that being the case, she held the greater right to sorrow.

"Stevie, go upstairs and get dressed. You're not a baby anymore. Everyone else has left for school. You're already late as it is."

Mary gave her father's words quiet consideration. Then, without looking at him, she stated flatly, "I'm not going to school ever again."

Andrew looked at her with surprise and amusement. It was at times like this that she seemed most like her mother. Still, she was only a child, and a very contrary child at that. "The choice isn't yours," he confirmed sharply. "I have to work. You can't stay home alone."

Rather than acknowledge him, she began drawing a butterfly on the damp window. She loved butterflies and was always amazed at how they emerged from a cocoon of darkness. "Can't Helen watch me?" she finally asked.

Andrew grew impatient. "Helen left for school. And even if she hadn't, she still couldn't stay home to watch after you."

"Dottie gets to stay home."

"Stevie, Dottie's only four years old. A neighbor lady's watching her." Before Andrew turned toward the kitchen, he gave his final orders: "Before you really make me angry, go upstairs and get dressed. Now!"

Mary shook her head as she stared back at her father. "No. I'm never going to school ever again. And I'm never going to any cemetery again."

"And I suppose you're never going to bathe again, or get dressed again?"

"Uh-uh."

Andrew felt the color rising in his face. He should spank her, but somehow he couldn't. Still, he couldn't risk pampering her. Louise had left him with six children to raise, and although Helen, age fourteen, and twelve-year-old Andrew were fairly self-sufficient, Muriel, Nelson, Mary, and Dottie, all ten and under, needed constant supervision. How, dear God, was he going to raise them? Where would he find the energy? These days he rarely felt up to the constant challenge of Mary's stubbornness. As a stevedore working Pennsylvania's Delaware River near Chester, employment was often scarce, wages low. It was the winter of 1928-29. With the nation headed for a depression, many Americans were already struggling to survive. Andrew prayed constantly that a turn into the '30s would be a triumph over the '20s. As it was, they had already become a family who had to hold onto things that many people threw away. At least when Louise was alive, his working the waters and being absent seemed to have had little effect on the children. Beyond being their children's stability, he could depend on Louise's budgeting skills to stretch his meager wages far enough to cover food, clothing, and rent. How had she done it? Now that Louise's domestic responsibilities were his, how could he both love his children and discipline them? Already he felt like an unbearable failure. Frustration coupled with irritation mounted as he turned on Mary. "You're the stubbornest child I've ever seen," Andrew said in a raised voice. "You either go upstairs and dress yourself, or I will dress you!"

Mary stomped out of the room and up the stairs. This battle with her father was a familiar version of past confrontations that had resulted in spankings. "Stevie," her mother had often lamented, "why do you push things to the extreme? Why not do what your daddy tells you from the start? Fighting the inevitable only makes it harder for you, and for me."

Mary glanced nervously around, as if she could hear her mother's reprimand. She did not want to be reminded of any trouble she might have been to her mother. Quickly she ran into the bedroom that she shared with her sisters and began dressing, an act that temporarily filled in the cracks of her grief. After putting on a wrinkled cotton dress, she layered it with hand-me-down sweaters from Helen and Muriel; the first sweater she pulled on was smaller than the second—a faded red wool that, despite numerous shrinkings, was big, baggy, and badly misshapen. Picking off some knotted fuzzballs, Mary licked them, rolled them between her thumb and finger, then stuck them on her hand. They looked like red sores.

She smiled slightly.

She walked into the bathroom and bandaged them, then went downstairs to show them to her father. Perhaps he would show her mercy when he saw her injury.

Andrew glanced up cautiously as his young daughter came into the kitchen. "Did you eat your oatmeal earlier?"

Mary shook her head no. "It was all lumpy. You don't make it like Mom did."

Once again Mary had caught him off guard. For a split second Andrew shifted into another world which included a warm kitchen with homey aromas . . . a kitchen with Louise. Now no matter how hard he tried, the kitchen seemed barren and cold without her. The cool disfavor with which his daughter was looking at him, as though she were a schoolteacher surveying a wayward student, made him uncomfortable. Haltingly he reminded Mary that Helen had made the oatmeal that morning.

Mary stood squarely before her father as she addressed him. "Then Helen doesn't make it like Mom either."

He felt a moment's strong desire to punish Mary for her insolence, but reminded himself again that she was grieving just as he was. However, he deliberately kept his voice stern when he said,

"You need to put on a jacket, scarf, galoshes, and some gloves."

She shoved her bandaged hand out. "I almost bled to death upstairs. I have a terrible cut."

Staring down at her hand, it was hard not to laugh, especially because he knew how much Mary loved bandages. In a wonderful way, Mary's use of drama to attract attention was charming. And at this particular moment, this trait of hers also provided her father a momentary relief from his sorrow. "Hmmm," Andrew said as he took her small hand in his, "I'm very glad that you survived such a disaster. Just how did you get such a terrible cut?"

Mary allowed her hand to be held, even gently caressed. "Well, I think a stranger cut me, someone from Delphia . . ."

"Philadelphia?"

"Yes."

"And what'd this stranger look like?"

"I don't know. He wore a . . . ah . . . a thing over his face, like a Halloween mask, and he told me in this awful voice that he was a stranger. And then he cut me. Did I tell you I almost bled to death?"

Andrew's voice changed from one of gentle amusement to curiosity. "Stevie, Stevie," he sighed heavily. "I certainly hope this imagination of yours is worth all the time that you put into it."

As he tied a woolen scarf around Mary's gold-brown hair which was cut square with bangs, his daughter's blue eyes widened, then misted over. "Daddy? Can't Mom come home for a visit at Christmas? If I talk to God and ask Him, won't God let her out of heaven to visit us?"

Andrew looked stricken. He was not a man of words; he could say little else to his children beyond explaining that Louise had died of tuberculosis and had gone to heaven to be with God. Once again he repeated this to his six-year-old daughter. "Your mother's with God, Stevie. But she'll always love us."

"Can she see us?"

"Yes—I mean, I hope so."

"But God won't let her visit us at Christmas?"

"No."

Mary sighed with exasperation. "But she really can see us, right?"

Andrew nodded as he bent to help Mary put on her coat.

"Even when," Mary paused, "—even when I'm taking my privacy?"

Andrew's brows raised in question.

Her voice lowered to a whisper. "You know, Daddy, when I have to go to the—you know," she paused. "I mean, Mom wouldn't want to look down on us then, especially down on Helen or Andy. They're sort of old to be seen during their privacy."

Mary couldn't understand why her father both laughed and cried as he hurried her out the front door and into the silently falling snow.

The snowflakes melted instantly as they met Mary's warm, turned-up nose. Elementary school was only two blocks away, but she deliberately trudged ahead slowly. Being in the first grade was boring. It had been fun at first until her teacher constantly claimed that she talked too much and reminded her that she shouldn't speak out of turn. "Listen more, talk less," had been the suggestion of everyone who knew her, including her own family. She shook her head wistfully. She had so much to say and no one wanted to listen to her!

The snow was falling gently, powdering over her footprints as quickly as she made them. Stopping, she looked down with wonder at the marks her galoshes had made in the virgin snow. Instead of walking, she began to jump two feet forward, then hopped on one foot to the right until it appeared that there were three footprints which gave the impression of a three-legged man. From that point she hopped on one foot, hoping that people would think a one-legged man had suddenly appeared. She kept up this game until she came to the stone church she and her family attended. Beyond iron gates stretched a courtyard where the snow was still untouched. She hopped forward to a point midway in the yard, then carefully lay down on her back in the snow. With a familiar determination, she moved her arms upward toward her head, then back down toward her side. As she lay there moving her arms up and down in wide sweeps, she heard crunching footsteps.

An older man dressed in a heavy black coat stared down at her. "A bit late for school aren't we, Miss Mary Stevenson?" the minister asked.

A myriad of excuses ran through her head, but she knew that making up stories to a priest might be as bad as fibbing to God and Jesus. Instead, she sat up and simply said, "I'm making a snow angel, Reverend."

Reaching down his hand to help her up, the Reverend smiled. He knew Mary well, found her delightful and humorous. He recalled the time she had heard that Jesus gave to the poor, and how, when the offering plate was passed around in church, she had helped herself. He was pleasantly surprised to find that the coins she had taken were not for her, but were given to those she considered less fortunate. It took a bit of fancy talking to explain that this was not exactly what Jesus had in mind. Still smiling, he looked at her snow angel. "It's a fine angel, indeed, that you've made, Mary." He tilted his head, then pointed to one of the angel's wings. "However, it's a bit off-center, wouldn't you say?"

Mary looked puzzled.

"The right wing," the minister explained. "It looks as though it's bent, like an angel with a broken wing."

By the time she reached school, Mary was filled with worry. She struggled with guilt. She could never recall being able to make a perfect angel. Somehow they all came out looking as though one of their wings was broken. All of her brothers and sisters made perfect angels. What was wrong with her?

"You're late again, Mary," her teacher reprimanded. Shrugging, Mary handed over the note that her father had written. "Go to the cloakroom and take off your coat and galoshes. You're dripping snow everywhere."

Still worried about her angel, Mary sat down on the cloakroom floor and pulled off her black rubber boots. Her shoes had caught inside, and after removing them from the galoshes, she had to put them back on. She tugged her gloves off carefully; perhaps the bandages on her hand would evoke sympathy from her teacher. She smiled and said hello to everyone as she reentered the classroom, stopping to have a short conversation with one of her friends. Only after her teacher asked her to take her seat and stop talking, did she quiet down.

Instead of listening to her teacher explain how ten minus seven equals three, she kept thinking of her angel with its broken wing. As she had often done, she began to silently speak to God. She may have talked too loudly to *people,* but she only spoke to *God* quietly in her mind. She loved God, and she wanted everybody to love Him, but since people didn't like listening to her, her relationship with Him was a secret greater than the one she kept about her broken-winged angel.

Life confused her and she fought to pierce its confusions. But God was not complex. God simply was. While some people seemed to struggle to know Him, this had never been a problem to Mary—at least not until He had taken her mother. When she talked to Him with her mind she felt His presence in the form of a golden light, a warmth that permeated all coldness, all darkness. She once told Him that she understood the pressures He was under being God, and she offered to help Him in any way. Still, she needed to know why, whenever she lay down in the snow to create an angel, did she become an angel with a broken wing? Her mind drifted.

"Mary! Are you listening to the lesson?" her teacher interrupted. Abruptly, Mary was brought back to the present. "You're daydreaming again, aren't you?"

Mary's eyes burned bright as she nodded yes. Her teacher struck the blackboard with a pointer. "Then perhaps you'd like to share your thoughts with the class, since they appear far more important than our lesson."

Mary slowly rose from her desk and looked around the room. "Well," she began as she focused on her teacher, "I was thinking about a poor, lonely farmer working outside in a bare field. He was a nice man, but he'd forgotten God, forgotten how to pray. He thought he could do everything by himself. Suddenly, much to his surprise, he saw something gold and shiny in the distance. At first the farmer thought it was a plane that had fallen from the sky, but as he rushed toward it, he saw that it wasn't a plane after all. It was an angel with a broken wing.

"As it began to rain and then to snow, the farmer wondered how he could fix this angel's broken wing. Should he glue it? Wire it back together? Use a piece of string? He was very poor and there wasn't much food in his house. He didn't know what to do, but he picked up the angel and carried her to safety and fed her a hot breakfast of oatmeal. It wasn't lumpy.

"He didn't have the money to call a doctor, and he didn't even know if doctors could fix an angel's broken wing, so all he could do was give the angel all he had. What he had was love, so he gave her love, and as he did, his love turned into golden light and wrapped itself around the angel's wing. Pretty soon the wing straightened out, and the angel gently kissed him on the forehead, then told him to take her to the highest hill. 'I've come to earth with a broken wing to help people find the love that's often hidden in their hearts. Even when you're downhearted, always look to the skies—to God—and know that your prayers'll be heard, that you're never alone.'

"'Will I see you again?' the farmer asked.

"'In a way. You'll feel me every time a golden butterfly gently brushes your cheek. You'll see my glow in a sunrise, my sparkle in every star that glitters. God's light is everywhere, all the time.' The angel paused. 'When we hear the bugle call, I'll take flight,' she added.

"With the angel beside him, the farmer learned to pray. Then the bugle called. The angel rose and spread her wings—perfect wings—and as the farmer watched, the angel soared upward toward earth's giant star. The sun started shining, and gold stardust sprinkled down, down, down. When the farmer looked out over his fields, vegetables that were ten times their normal size broke through the empty ground. And from that day until forever, whenever the farmer felt downhearted, he fell to his knees and looked up toward the skies, always turning to God in time of trouble, always thanking God for blessings given.

"And sometimes—sometimes—the farmer thought that he felt the gentle brush of a butterfly's wings."

A hush had quieted the class. Mary's teacher stood near the door and looked intently at this young child and thought, "She doesn't listen to me, nor to her family. But this renegade angel obviously listens to something—or someone."

White Cracker

"Some people with great virtues are disagreeable, while others with great vices are delightful."
—*Duc de La Rochefoucauld*

IT HAD BEEN SNOWING all day, which meant there would be no recess. By the time the lunch bell sounded Mary had become uneasily aware of the whispering around her, but it was not until she leaned down to take a sip of water at the fountain that the truth hit her: she was the subject of their whispers!

"Don't drink out of that fountain now. Stevenson's contagious. Her family's diseased."

Mary stared blankly at one of her classmates, and then she squinted as she remembered something she had overheard earlier, something so unpleasant that it had not been openly discussed within her home.

The "unspeakable" had to do with the disease that had claimed her mother. At the thought of her beloved mom, Mary lost her timidity. Angrily she challenged one of her tormentors. "My family is not diseased!"

Her schoolmates' eyes studied her. "Your mother died of TB! Your house was under quarantine!"

"But I'm not diseased."

An older student laughed in knowing delight, then began to sing, "TB or not TB, that is the congestion. Consumption be done about it? Of cough not, of cough not, not for a lung, lung time."

If she had not liked school before, Mary now found it a horrible place to be. Whenever she felt a normal cough coming on, she would hold her breath until her cheeks turned scarlet. She was glad when spring arrived because it was easier to skip school when the weather was warm. Being outside in the cold was almost worse than being in the schoolroom.

Springtime also meant dance time. Ever since she turned three Mary had danced on the street corners with the black children. She loved the rhythm, loved Friday nights when a portion of Kerlin Street was blocked off for street dancing, even loved the fact that she was called "White Cracker" by her black friends. It was a term used with affection, and when people threw pennies at her and yelled, "Dance, White Cracker, dance," she would dance until she dropped.

A black girl accompanied her on the harmonica, playing the only two tunes she knew, "Sweet Georgia Brown" and "Swanee River." Later in the evening, when the older folks joined the festivities, Ethel Waters would sing.

Ethel had gone to school with Mary's father and lived nearby. "You dance mighty fine, little Miss White Cracker," Ethel Waters would praise as she handed Mary a cookie.

"Thank you, ma'am," Mary would answer shyly.

Occasionally Duke Ellington joined in and played a piano that had been lowered onto the street. The Duke was a cousin of the woman who often cared for Dottie and Mary when her father was working the waters. She would never have guessed that these two people would someday be world famous. All she knew was that she loved them both, loved how they clapped for her, how they threw pennies—sometimes nickels and dimes—to see her dance.

With the money, she went to see shows at the Apollo Theater. Starry-eyed, she watched the antics of Buster Keaton, then went home and reenacted what she had seen on the screen for her sisters and brothers. Although they laughed, she often felt a nameless resentment in the air. She knew there was something about her that was not like them, something about her that insisted upon being the center of attention. "Do you always have to dance on street corners?" was a question people were always asking. "Why are you always drawing attention to yourself? Can't you direct some of that energy toward your studies?"

Mary tried, but the truth was she could see nothing valuable in attending school, especially a school where people whispered and pointed fingers at her. At first the teasing had to do with her mother's disease—later, the misshapen clothing she wore. When her father was home she had to be in bed before the sun went down, so attending school cut into her hours for fun. Of course summer was a different story. Summer meant complete freedom. School was out, which meant that she had her sisters and brothers to play with, especially her brothers, who liked having fun even more than she did.

Mary sometimes earned money for fun in unorthodox ways. One summer afternoon while taking her doll for a stroll she noticed a sign over a bin outside a store that said, "Help Yourself."

"How wonderful," Mary said as she inspected the bin of shoes. She happily loaded shoes into her doll carriage and headed for home. Her large blue eyes were lively as she unloaded her haul and hooked up Nelson's wagon to the back of the carriage for a second and larger load. Then she carefully matched each shoe to its mate and set them out on the front yard of her home with a sign that read, "Nu Shoos 4 Sail 25 sents a pare."

The light was ebbing by the time she closed up shop. Her father would be home soon and she had to be in the house. Later, after going to bed, she was awakened by her father. Trying to focus on him, she sleepily asked what was wrong?

"There's a woman waiting outside our front door asking if you have any shoes left for sale," he replied, his voice filled with curiosity.

Mary shifted her glance to a corner of the bedroom. "I have three pairs left," she announced proudly.

"And where did you get these shoes, young lady?" Andrew inquired sternly.

"The dime store was giving them away for free," she explained. "I'm going to give some of the money I make to the poor."

"Why would the store give shoes away?"

Mary shrugged. "I don't know, Daddy. They just put up a sign that said 'Help Yourself,' so I did. Don't you think I did good?"

Slapping his forehead with the palm of his hand, Andrew replied, "I think I'd better call your uncle at the police station."

Mary looked up at her father silently. Finally she asked, "Did I break the law? Am I going to jail?"

Andrew smiled and shook his head. "I doubt it. But this is something that has to be straightened out."

The next day when her uncle came over to hear what she had done, he laughed. "Oh, Stevie," he lamented. "Only you!"

She thought dimly that his words were echoes of a constant theme in their household: "Oh, Stevie, only you!" Why was she so different?

The man who owned the store was understanding. "I've got to admit," he said as he tousled Mary's hair, "my sign was misleading."

When the story made the newspapers, several people in Mary's school who were wearing new shoes (including the school nurse) stopped their whispers long enough to thank her. The nation was suffering a financial depression; new shoes were hard to come by, and Mary's misunderstanding had become a bounty to many.

Not long after, Mary did break a law, but again, not knowingly. A man who had read the shoe story in the newspaper approached Mary as she was strolling with her doll carriage. "How'd you like to earn a nickel or a dime delivering bottles to people in your neighborhood?"

She thought for a few moments, then answered, "Sure, Mister."

Cautiously the man looked around before placing a bottle wrapped in old newspaper in the carriage. "Do you know the McConnells?" he whispered.

"Sure. They live two doors down from me."

The man's voice lowered. "Deliver this to them. They'll give you an envelope for me. I'll meet you back here in fifteen minutes. When you bring me back the envelope I'll give you a nickel."

Mary liked the idea of earning money and using that money to help her family. "Okay," she answered eagerly.

"And," he added quickly, "this is our secret. You can't tell anyone."

"Why?"

"Because if the other kids knew, they'd cut into your territory. Then you'd get nothing."

Her tiny mouth bowed in contemplation. "I don't mind sharing. It's the thing to do."

The man looked at her in astonishment. "Yeah. Well, maybe later. But right now we gotta keep this business deal between us."

Mary agreed. As she walked rapidly toward the McConnell's house, she wondered what was wrapped inside the newspaper. No one on the street paid any attention to her and the delivery went off smoothly. However, she wondered why Mr. McConnell was nervous when he handed her the sealed envelope. On the way back to deliver it to the man who said he would pay her the nickel, she ran into her uncle who was in his police uniform.

"Afternoon, Stevie. What're you doing today?"

"I delivered a package to someone." Turning around, she pointed to the man standing across the street. "For that man. He's paying me a nickel."

Her uncle bolted toward the man, but he ran out of sight. Instead of giving chase, her uncle turned back to her. When she handed her uncle the envelope, he kneeled down in front of her and explained, "This is bootleg money, Stevie."

Her first thought was: Oh, no! Not illegal shoes again! Boot, after all, meant a work shoe like her father wore, and leg—well a leg was something attached to a foot which wore a boot! It was years before she came to understand what "bootlegging" really was.

Later in hot July, a golden sun tanned Mary's face, and her eyes were the exact color of the summer sky. Even her smile suggested a late summer morning. Suddenly the door behind her opened, and Andy and Nelson came bounding out onto the porch and down the steps. "Where're you going?" she asked.

Not looking at her, Nelson yelled back, "We're going pole-jumping."

Mary followed her brothers as they ran around the corner and down the alley toward the backyard. "What's pole-jumping?" she asked breathlessly.

Andy slowed his pace as his eyes swept over his younger sister. "Pole-jumping's not for little girls, Stevie. You're always following us. Go back out front."

Mary's young face filled with obstinance. "Not until you tell me what pole-jumping is and why it's not for girls!"

Andy smiled slightly. "Okay. Pole-jumping's when you nail two wooden clothesline props together. Then you run across that straight roof up there, then the slanted one. At the end of the slanted roof you have to jab the props into the ground real hard in order to fly over the tack shed."

Mary's eyes brightened. "Let me see you do it." Andy hesitated.

"I dare you," Mary insisted.

Chuckling, Andy glanced sidelong at his sister, who was egging him on. "Sure."

After Andy successfully vaulted the tack shed at the end of the yard, Nelson took his turn. With the heated gold of the sun shimmering in the top of a tree and on the rooftops, Mary watched them carefully, contemplating their smooth movements. "I want to do it. I know how."

"You're too young," Andy said firmly.

"How young were you when you first tried it?"

Andy bowed his head in thought. "You're a girl . . ."

"Yeah," Nelson added. "Pole-jumping's not for girls."

Mary put her hands on her hips. "Who says?"

"It's a law," Nelson retorted, then paused. "I think it is, isn't it, Andy?"

"Does Daddy know you pole-jump?" Mary asked, already suspecting the answer. Andy and Nelson glanced at each other nervously. "I'll tell him. Unless . . . "

"Unless what?" Andy asked forlornly.

"You let me try."

Mary's threat hit home. They knew she would tell if she didn't get her way. "All right, if you'll promise not to tell anyone."

Coloring with excitement, Mary nodded, then climbed atop the flat roof. She ran across it with ease, but apparently the boys had forgotten how much lighter she was than they were. She flew over the tack shed, out across the alley, hit an iron rung on a telephone pole, then hit a metal garbage can on the way down. She woke in the hospital with her arm broken, her foot fractured, and her chin split open. Her father sat beside her bed, his face a mixture of tension, concern, and anger. "How'd this happen?" he asked.

Andy and Nelson hovered in the background, uncertain and worried. Mary's eyes locked with theirs. A slight trembling ran through her warm cheeks and hands. Turning to her father she said, "I climbed the telephone pole and fell."

Andrew studied his daughter as he tried to catch any hesitation in her voice. But there was none. Her tone was even and honest. He turned around and stared at his sons, but, despite his initial instincts, there was nothing in their expressions to contradict Mary's story. He looked back at Mary. "Well, Stevie," he sighed heavily, "I guess I don't have to tell you that pole-climbing, or even tree-climbing, is dangerous."

"I know," Mary replied in a faint and empty voice. "I won't do it again, Daddy."

When her father temporarily left her room, Andy and Nelson came to her. "Thanks for not telling on us, Stevie," they both said.

Mary simpered and made a weak little gesture with her left hand. "You're welcome, Andy. It's not your fault, even though you should have stopped me since I'm your little sister—and since I'm just a girl."

Andy smiled painfully. "Yeah. I know. I feel rotten about this."

Mary's eyes widened and sparkled. "You probably would feel a lot better if you bought me an ice cream cone every day."

Andy backed up quickly. "Every day?"

"Not forever," Mary said in a faint voice. "Only until I can use my right arm again, and until I walk again—*if* I ever walk again."

Using her cast arm to advantage as long as possible, Mary hobbled around. When her foot healed she decided that it was time for her arm to heal. She enjoyed the ice cream cones, but it was not worth endless confinement, despite the fact that school had once again begun. Because of the lack of food in the house, there was something to be said in favor of school, or rather, the free school lunches. When her father was home there was hot stew and fresh milk, but when he was away Helen often stood each of them on a chair in front of the sink so they could drink enough water to fill their stomachs. Sometimes they would suck on pieces of plaster from the attic wall. If they were lucky, somebody in the neighborhood would get a new roof, and when the workmen left for lunch, they would chew on the tar. Now the neighborhood children had an excuse to call the Stevensons a new name: "Tar Babies."

When winter came, Mary and her brothers and sisters mixed snow and vanilla together for ice cream and melted icicles for water when the pipes froze. When the weather warmed up, Mary danced again on the street corners.

"This is getting embarrassing," Andy told her. "You're making a spectacle of yourself."

"I earned three dollars tonight," Mary said. "That's enough to buy us food."

Andy stared at the money with amazement.

"Count it."

Andy counted the coins. "Three dollars to the penny."

Andy looked down at his sister. He was intrigued by the money, but still critical. The only one in the family who seemed to approve of Mary was Nelson. Her energy fascinated him. He seldom knew where Stevie was coming from—and he never knew where she was going! Nelson believed that Mary would make a splendid entertainer. He alone understood her, and he constantly stood up for her and sometimes even covered for her.

Sometimes after Andy and Nelson had bedded down in the attic, they had quiet discussions about Mary becoming a professional entertainer, and to a point, Andy agreed with his brother. There *was* something out of the ordinary about little Mary. And after all, it was clear that she hated school, with its formal and rigid studies. So what else could she become? What else could she do with her life other than entertain people?

"So what do you say now?" Mary asked, as she took her money back from Andy.

Andy smiled a little before answering his sister. "What do I have to say about your earning three dollars? I say, dance, White Cracker, dance!"

Bridges

MARY COULD NOT UNDERSTAND her father's transformation, as he went from his usual blandness to a sudden tone of open shock in his voice. Andrew Stevenson was very reserved and believed that showing any emotion demonstrated vulnerability and weakness. He despised emotional displays as much as he hated laziness and disrespect. Yet at that precise moment as her father stood at their front door listening to a policeman, strange patterns of his voice, devastated with open grief, floated in and out of Mary's hearing. When Andrew closed the door and turned toward Mary and Dottie, his face was white. He began to speak, but suddenly stopped in order to control the trembling of his lips.

Ten-year-old Mary waited. "Daddy . . . ?" she asked tentatively.

He turned to stare at her. Standing in the middle of the living room in his work clothes he seemed frozen, unable to move or speak. Finally, with lips still trembling, he gave Mary a quiet but firm order: "Go find Helen, Andrew, and Muriel. Quickly."

"Should I find Nelson too?"

It seemed a long while before he could answer her. "No, Stevie," he uttered in a strained voice. "Do as I say. Now."

When she found her brothers and sisters, they gathered in the living room and sat watching their father's face. If they expected to be reprimanded, what they experienced instead was a heaviness that kept their father silent. No one moved. The children barely breathed.

After a while, their father turned and sat down by a window, apart from the others. He looked at them blankly and then began to speak. Never before, not even when her mother had died four years earlier, had Mary heard so much pain in her father's voice. "Nelson was walking across the Third Street Bridge. I don't know how it happened, but he fell off. He hit a piece of metal under the bridge which apparently cut open his back. He drowned in the river below."

Mary hugged Dottie close to her, then stared in turn at Helen, at Andrew, at Muriel. A jingle of a bracelet interrupted the breathless quiet. Outside, the sound of a truck motor, human voices, the clicking of a typewriter seemed a stark contrast to the unreality inside their home.

Then Mary heard the sound of sobbing. One of her sisters? Her own? She was not sure. She was only dimly aware of anything. What did her father mean? Why was he saying this horrible thing? Finally, she shook her head. "Oh, but Daddy, you're wrong! I saw Nelson in the alley a little while ago."

Andrew looked at Mary. She seemed wounded by anything he did or said. His sense of exhaustion was growing, but he owed his children the truth, no matter how brutal it was. He no more had it in him to cushion their pain than to make them believe that life was full of joy. Life was simply a constant struggle. Death was an end to that struggle.

"I'm sorry, Stevie. But Nelson is dead. We'll bury him beside your mother."

Mary sat hunched as though she needed a hole to shrink into. She looked up at her father with pleading eyes, and as he nodded with grim reaffirmation, she knew that Nelson was truly dead. From that moment her struggle was no longer against the words he spoke but with how to live her life without Nelson.

In awed admiration, she had clung to Nelson for years. She had come to him for advice, for protection, for loans—for ice cream cones. She was closer to him than to any of them. He had made her believe in herself; his advice and attention had given her living transfusions of hope and vitality.

Mary glanced downward, as if debating a bigger truth than simply death, and as her young mind struggled under the load of life's enigmas, she turned in her mind to God. He must understand all this, but she surely didn't. She looked around at her family, saw their bewilderment, unhappiness, and helplessness, and asked God to help them. For a split second she was filled with a joyous, boundless power that needed sharing—a warmth that was overpowering. She must make them feel it too—but how?

Eventually, after more long absences from school, the principal expelled her. Her hope that her father would allow her to stay out of school was a wish without foundation. He immediately enrolled her in another school across town. "Let's see how you like a walk to school that's ten times longer than before," he said angrily.

"Do I really *have* to go to school?" she pleaded. "Let me stay home and I'll clean the house and cook and—"

"You have to attend school, Stevie. It's the law. My law!"

What sort of misery did her father wish upon her, she lamented as she trudged slowly toward her new school. Why was he, and the rest of her family, always so disappointed in her? If only Nelson were here! He had taken the gray and the ugly and turned it golden and beautiful. Suddenly the thought of Nelson filled her with energy and she began to run with a strength she had never known before. It was as if she were the wind and Nelson the sky. She felt like a butterfly emerging from its cocoon of darkness.

The run became so pleasant that she enjoyed going to school, and when someone saw how fast she ran, she was picked to race on the school's relay team. Because of her, her team won top awards. Winning was so much fun! And so was school now that she was a hero.

When she showed her medal to her father, he sighed, then said with idle disinterest, "I'm glad that you like school, Stevie, but your grades need improvement. Running relays'll do nothing to help you in the future. You need to think about your priorities. Be more attentive in school like Helen and Muriel. Even Dottie does better with her lessons than you do. You need to prepare yourself for the dog-eat-dog competition of this world."

Mary's face turned sullen. "I like to write poetry, Daddy. You've read some of the things I've written, and you like them."

"Yes, and I've often wondered where you get some of your thoughts."

"From God," Mary said without hesitation.

There was a moment's pause. "Listen, Stevie," her father began heavily. "Poetry has its place. And I'm not surprised that you like to write poetry since you're a descendant of Robert Louis Stevenson."

"Tell me about him again," Mary asked eagerly.

"There's not much to tell, other than he was a very great Scottish poet from my side of the family. He died nearly thirty years before you were born, but you resemble him in a way."

Mary's eyes widened. "I do?"

"Not in the physical sense. But in your simple, reverent view of the world."

"Isn't that good?"

"No, not particularly," Andrew drawled. "Such a view's unrealistic. There are very few rich poets. Poetry's nice to read, but essentially it's just rambling words on a piece of paper."

For a moment Mary had little else to say. Her ideas always seemed to become a family contest. Still, her ancestors were her rightful inheritance. "Daddy, Robert Louis Stevenson's words are more than just words on a piece of paper. He's read by the entire world."

Andrew fumbled irritably with his work shirt collar. He had not intended to get into another debate with Mary, even though at fourteen she had a certain entitlement to her own ideas and opinions. "Stevie, be realistic. Do you actually think that you have the talent to write a poem that could someday be read by the entire world?"

At age fourteen, having made it through the eighth grade, Mary called it quits. Her father seemed resigned but disappointed, and at last he ceased arguing. There was sadness in his eyes when he looked at her. She had been six years old when her mother had died, only ten when Nelson had drowned. Had they lived he was sure that she would have chosen to be better armed before entering the adult world. Still, she was only fourteen, and he was her father. If she thought that she could do as she wished, she would soon discover otherwise. He did not enjoy being her adversary, but someone had to keep her restless nature in check.

Andrew Stevenson *was* in charge and let that fact be understood through words and physical punishments. That he was gone a great deal of the time did not mean he was not in control, as he would remind Mary when he was home. "I only wish that you'd follow the paths of your older sisters. They're studying to be nurse's aides, a very respectable profession. They'll make their mark on the world . . . while you? All you seem to do is play, and disobey."

Mary was filled with guilt as she watched her father shake his head angrily. What would he say if he knew that she had accepted a date to go to the circus with a boy named Gerry without asking his permission?

Well, she sighed, she would simply have to deal with that later. Right now her concern was what to wear and what to say to Gerry in order to appear intelligent. In between trying on various outfits, some belonging to her sisters, she engaged in imaginary conversations with Gerry—conversations ranging from, "Well, Gerry, just what is your opinion concerning President Roosevelt's New Deal?" to, "Don't you just love Ovaltine?"

When Gerry arrived the following Saturday afternoon, Mary was dressed in a brown skirt, yellow blouse, and brown-and-white saddle shoes. Gerry wore brown pants, a yellow shirt, and brown-and-white saddle shoes. Mary chuckled. They looked like matching bookends!

More nervous than ever, Mary greeted Gerry before he had time to knock on the front door and wake her father from his nap. Standing outside on the porch, she paused and looked up and down the street. Before Gerry had time to respond to her cheery hello she blurted out, "Tell me, what's your opinion concerning President Roosevelt's love of Ovaltine?"

Gerry stared at her blankly. It was like being asked if he walked to work or carried his lunch. Still, he was amused by her question, and he also thought she was very pretty. He was about five inches taller than Mary, which made him feel very protective. As he took her arm to lead her down the steps, an upstairs bedroom window opened. A man leaned out and began shouting.

"What's going on down there?" Andrew Stevenson hollered.

Mary whispered, "Gerry, move away from me. That's my father." Looking upward, Mary sucked in her breath. "This is Gerry, Daddy. He's taking me to the circus. We won't be late."

Andrew looked down at her blankly. "What?"

"I said—"

"I heard what you said. Now you hear what I'm saying: You are *not* going to the circus. You're too young for boys!"

Closing her eyes in order to stop the gathering tears, Mary shook her head, then looked at Gerry. "I'm sorry, Gerry. I forgot to ask Daddy. Maybe another time?"

A faint glow was streaming from behind the buildings in the sky. Mary liked to imagine it was the golden breath of a city that would soon find peace. To find peace, Mary thought, and to find joy somewhere would be like having Christmas in summer.

Every evening before the sun went down, she would sit on the front steps and talk with her friend Maria about happiness and boys, especially boys. Maria had to wear a brace on her leg, but that didn't keep the two from constantly plotting ways to outwit their strict parents and go dancing.

Going dancing and meeting boys was all Mary wanted except to fill that sudden, peculiar urge she often had to put her thoughts down on paper, especially in times of emptiness. She felt so immobile, as if nothing was ever going to happen in her life, as if time had stood still and that she, because of being fourteen, was caught up in the parenthesis of living. Living in fear of her father's wrath left her feeling helpless. She wanted to be the motivating power of her own happiness, not simply a spectator. She also wanted to feel herself carried by the power of some achievement, but what? "The only talent I have is my dancing," she admitted to Maria. "And Daddy forbids me to go anyplace near music."

"Want to go on a moonlight dance on the cruise ship called *The Wilson Line?*" Maria asked mischievously.

"What're you talking about?"

"I've met a fellow named Joe and he has a friend named Bill. I told him about you. They want us to go on this dance cruise Friday night. I said that we'd have to meet them someplace else besides our houses, maybe in the alley. So, how about it?"

Mary pursed her lips. "I don't know . . ."

"Don't be so afraid of your father. Fear is dull."

Glancing at her friend slyly, Mary's voice took on a livelier, bolder tone. "You're right. I'll pretend I'm going to bed early, then I'll get dressed. I've been good for so long that Daddy thinks he's got me beat. Plus, he doesn't seem to notice anything I'm doing anymore."

"Be careful though, Stevie. You know what they say about being too confident."

Mary knew what Maria meant. "Daddy comes home so tired that he falls asleep early in his chair. You could light a fire under him and he wouldn't budge. But, I'll be careful. The toughest part'll be sneaking back in. I've got to be sure a door's unlocked."

From a cousin, Mary borrowed a red crepe dress which sheathed her figure tightly, widening in a mass of material below the knee line. She also "borrowed" a tube of red lipstick from one of her sisters. Because nylons were expensive and scarce, Mary drew a black seam down the back of her legs with coal; then she smeared some of the coal on her fingers and used it as eye shadow. Her fair hair, abundant and beautifully brushed, framed a face with impressive lashes, blue eyes, and naturally good skin color.

Intrigued by the reflection staring back at her in the mirror, Mary's face turned lively and coquettish as her eyes flashed with secrecy. She sighed and smiled. Turning, she looked at Dottie asleep across the bed and clicked off the small bureau lamp. Just in case her father checked on her in the darkened bedroom, she gently padded the bed and pulled the covers up around her pillow to give the impression that she, too, was asleep. Helen, Muriel, and Andy, all old enough to go out on Friday nights, had already left.

Earlier Mary had unlocked the back door, and for good measure, she also unlocked a kitchen window so she could sneak back in. Carefully, she opened the bedroom door, closing it silently behind her. As she tiptoed down the stairs, she was overcome by fear at the risk she was taking. Stopping, she sucked in her breath and listened for her father's familiar snoring from the living-room chair where he always fell asleep. She tiptoed toward the door and out onto the porch, where, after a few seconds of trying to still her pounding heart, she peeked through the living-room window. Her father was sleeping undisturbed, and her terror began to subside.

Maria, Joe, and Bill were waiting for her at the end of the alley. After introductions Bill's admiring eyes reassured her that she looked wonderful. She smiled at him demurely. Joe drove them to Chester where they boarded the ship, and Mary's breathing finally fell into a normal pattern. Once the ship pulled out from its second stop in Philadelphia, the music began, and with it her reticence disappeared. She danced every number from "Begin the Beguine" to the "Jersey Bounce."

"I'd like to see more of you, Mary," Bill said as the hour grew late. "Is that possible?"

As her eyes dropped, she thought of how cute he looked in the sailor hat cocked on the back of his head. "Well, yes, but secretly. My father's very strict."

At about the same time that Bill told her that he loved how her eyes deepened in color as the night darkened, the ship's whistle sounded that the cruise was over. As they walked down the gangplank in Chester, Mary's father stepped out of the darkness and gave her the hardest slap she had ever received in her entire life.

"Daddy . . . I . . . ." He hit her again, and she screamed. Shaking and crying, she turned and began running down the street and across the drawbridge. By the time she was on the middle of the bridge her frenzied sobs made her stagger, and she fell. Suddenly, the light on the bridge turned red, and as it began to draw up in order to allow a ship to pass, she knew that she was trapped in the middle. Tears ran down her cheeks as she looked around helplessly. She knew that at any moment she might fall, like Nelson had, into the dark swirling waters. As she clung to the metal rail, sheets of rain began falling, drenching her, shrinking her dress and causing its red dye to run down her arms and legs while the coal-black eye shadow made inky trails down her face. She screamed in terror.

Closing her eyes tightly she thought of Nelson and God simultaneously. Somewhere in her paralyzed mind she heard someone say, "Hang on, Stevie, hang on."

After being trapped high above the Delaware River for what seemed an eternity, but was in reality around fifteen minutes, the bridge lowered again. Dazed, she released her hold and fell to her knees, drained of emotion. Once the bridge was in place she ran from her father, beating him home only by minutes. Wet and miserable, she crawled into bed beside the still-sleeping Dottie. Wanting to cry more than ever, all she could do was draw up into a ball and pray that her horror had been a nightmare. The light flicked on. Her father stood over her in a rage. Mary drew further into herself, but as he jerked her out of bed, she realized there was no escape into fantasy. He hit her so hard that both her earrings flew off. "Who do you think you are?" he shouted. "You are not of age; you are not allowed to date! I'm your father and what I say, goes!"

The sharpness of his slap made her head dizzy. "Daddy, please," she begged. "Please don't hit me again! It was only an innocent dance."

Her explanation was like pouring gasoline on a fire. "Innocent dance! Hanging on for your life over a river in the dead of night is only an innocent dance! Did you want to end up like Nelson?"

Somehow the reminder of Nelson infuriated her father still more, and he threw Mary down the stairs. Before she could get up he ran after her, picked her up, opened the cellar door and ordered her down into the musty darkness, locking the door behind her. "Did it ever occur to you that nighttime is dangerous for a young girl like you?" he continued to shout from above. "No boys, no lying, no sneaking out! You're a child. I'm your father, and you will not disobey me!"

Finally she was left alone with the silence broken only by the sound of rats scurrying about. Freezing in her wet clothes, she tried to warm herself by fanning the flame of the hatred she felt toward her father. She was unable to consider the possibility that her father's anger was born of fear and concern for her—but how could someone so young understand such a complex thing?

"God, where are you?" Mary pleaded. "Why did you let this happen to me?" Her mind turned to her mother and Nelson, and her longing for them grew until her heart held nothing but pain. Had they been around they would have protected her. But they were gone. And she must get away as well. No matter what she had to do, somehow she had to get away.

WHEN GOD PUSHED THE PENCIL

"Genius is the ability to reduce the complicated to the simple." —C. W. Ceram

IT HAD BEEN SNOWING for several days, and once again it appeared that the world had folded its wings. As the wind whipped the snow around her, icy flakes whirled into Mary's face with a biting kiss, clinging to her cheeks and hair in small clumps.

She was locked out of her house. Everyone had been gone when she got home, including her father who was working the dry docks. She did not even have school as a place of refuge.

A tear rolled down her cheek as the harsh fingers of the wind stung her face. Her father's treatment the night of the dance had been brutal. She didn't feel she'd deserved to be beaten and locked in a cold basement. Didn't he realize she was no longer a child? Still, she was not an adult either. She was in limbo, and she wondered why she lived and whether, in the end, her existence made any difference.

Hugging thin arms around her frail body, she tried to imagine a comfortable place to curl up. She imagined the sweet smell of apple pie baking in a hot oven, how it would feel to be in a warm room watching the icy snow through parted lace curtains.

Despite her pleas that fourteen was old enough to date, the truth was that fourteen was too young to be so alone. Even though her father, three sisters, and brother existed a breath away, the death of her mother and Nelson had left such an emptiness that she had felt like an orphan.

Old memories of family images danced around her like a sweet melody played on a piano with dusty keys. "I miss you so much, Mom," she whispered. "Why did you die and leave me?"

As the wind's tempo increased, its sound took on varied tones: some sharp, some soft. If she closed her eyes the tones became the sound of a whistling kettle. She could smell the homey air of her mother's kitchen, a kitchen scented by fresh ground coffee and baked ham. When her mother was alive, this empty house had been a cozy home that stood quiet in the sun yet creaked at night as it settled into sleepy comfort, a home with rooms that during the day rang with the shouts and games of children.

"Daddy wouldn't have beaten me, Mom," she whispered, "if you had lived."

Overshadowing her grief was the constant poverty and hunger. She was so tired of always being poor, of always wanting and never having. Could she ever escape from hunger? Wasn't there someone out there who would rescue her?

She looked upward, pleading, "God, why have you allowed all of this to happen? Why did you take Mom and Nelson from me? What have I ever done to make you so angry?"

Questioning God seemed an act of rebellion against someone whom she dearly loved. Like the air that she breathed and like the golden sun that she longed for, she rarely felt separated from God, or out of His sight. God had always been as much a part of her physical being as the heart that beat within her chest. Because she had never viewed God as separate from her, it was no more necessary to talk about Him than was it necessary to brag that she had a heart that beat.

God *was,* and because He was, she thought that everyone knew Him as she did. Her faith had never been a mysterious alleyway through which she had to pass in order to see His Light. He was as much a part of her family as were her brothers and sisters. Perhaps even more so.

She often found herself conversing with God on all levels: from deep love to outrageous anger. One time she promised God that she would not blackmail her brothers, which had been followed by a smile and a whisper of, "Unless, of course they need to be taught a lesson, or if there might be an ice cream cone involved."

For as long as she could remember, her approach to God had been one of great familiarity, a sort of familial love. Her mind had not been cluttered with unnecessary pockets of prejudice, perhaps because she had been raised by blacks and whites alike. She knew that God had no color but was a being of "Light." She believed that when God created man in His image that it meant that God gave of His Light in the form of a new soul. The soul needed the human body in order to have experience and growth, but the soul itself had neither color nor wrinkles. In her mind's eye God's creations had been so masterfully coordinated that they moved to some tremendous cosmic rhythm that only the soul could hear.

She also felt that rather than man having a soul, the truth was that physical life was the soul having a human experience. She knew all of this, believed all of this, knew that when she wrote poetry that it was God who pushed her pencil. Still, if she truly knew all of this then why was she now criticizing and questioning God? Wasn't this a sign of doubt? And in doubting wouldn't she go to hell?

She felt her body tremble from both the cold and her doubts, but rather than immediately surrender to apologizing to Him, her mind traveled backward to another cold winter.

It had been the first Christmas without her mother. The snowflakes, a grayish wet, had melted instantly as they met with her warm cheeks. Her woolen hat had shrunk from too much wear and too many washings. Her coat was a faded hand-me-down with two missing buttons, and she wore only one glove. Somehow she had lost its mate. Yet this day was not sad—school was out for the holidays and so her steps were bouncy as she skipped down the wooden stairs that led to the sidewalk. Smiling with confidence, she turned to look back at her house, where in the summer conversations drifted easily from porch to porch.

She imagined a Christmas tree in the front window.

As she walked down the street and around the corner, she sniffed the pine-scented air of Christmas, listened to the endless carols, noticed the green wreaths dotted by red holly berries that hung everywhere, even on lamp posts. Homes and stores alike boasted electric candles which awaited winter's early nightfall in which to glow. It was all so exciting.

Her breath caught and her heart stopped as she neared a large store. Inside was the largest Christmas tree she had ever seen. It reached up and beyond the second story and was topped by a magnificent star. Sitting beneath the tree in a large, ornate chair was—*him.*

If God answered daily prayers, surely this bearded man in a red suit was the one God had designated to answer mundane ones—like making certain the Stevensons had a Christmas tree.

The line was long and slow moving. The longer she waited the more frightened she became. She bit her bottom lip, hoping to push the fear away. She must get hold of herself in order to tell him about her needs for a tree. Wouldn't the line ever move? Halfway, she felt her bladder ache but rather than chance losing her place, she began twisting and turning. Miraculously the discomfort disappeared by the time her turn had come.

Awestruck by his white beard and twinkling blue eyes, she could barely answer when he asked her name. "Don't you know?" she had quizzed.

Laughing, he shook his head. "Of course. But it's our secret. Right?"

She nodded.

"So, what would you like for Christmas?"

"A wonderful Christmas tree with silvery tinsel. The kind that we had when my mother was alive."

He looked down at her. "Won't your father buy you a tree?"

She shrugged. "I think he might say it was a waste of money. We need food, things like that."

Noting how his lips faintly drew inward, she suffered a sudden feeling that maybe he wasn't the real thing but an imposter. Still, it would be impolite to ask.

"Isn't there a special present that you want?"

She looked at his glowing beard and red suit as she leaned into his full-framed body. "Presents happen when you have a tree. If you don't have a tree, then there aren't presents." Pausing, she drew back her head and smiled. "So will you bring me the tree?"

His face went blank and he closed his eyes. His movements, as he removed her from his lap, were gentle. 'I'll do my very best," he promised.

Going to sleep Christmas Eve had been nearly impossible. As she snuggled up against Dottie beneath an old quilt, she listened intently for the jingle of sleigh bells or the pawing of hooves. Over and over she jumped from bed and ran to the window. Where was he?

Then it dawned on her that this magical man might not come to her house if she remained awake. She willed herself into a fitful sleep. She awoke with a start. By the faded light she knew that it was early morning—Christmas morning. Rather than remember that Christmas was the celebration of Jesus' birth, she could only wonder whether the tree had been delivered. Quietly she tiptoed out of bed, down the creaky stairs, and into the living room. Nothing had changed. There was no Christmas tree, nothing. Frantically, she ran to the window and looking upward, watched the morning sun push night into the past. Holding back the tears until her throat ached, she asked, "Why?"

The day before New Year's Eve she found an amazing bounty that had been abandoned along the curbside. The large tree still had silvery tinsel entwined in its limbs, blowing in the icy wind.

By the time she had dragged the tree home, her hands were red and raw. The real problem would be how to drag the tree up the steps, across the porch, and into her house? She knew that somehow she had to place it in front of the window.

Santa may not have left town yet.

Half the branches bent as she shoved and pulled the tree through the front door.

"Stevie," her father asked, "what're you doing?"

"I found our Christmas tree, Daddy. Maybe it's not too late."

Her father's voice softened slightly. "No. Christmas has come and gone. Take that tree back to the curb. Its needles are already falling. Maybe next year."

Instead of doing as her father had ordered, she dragged the tree toward the cemetery. Perhaps if she buried it straight up in the snow, she could save it for the following Christmas. After leaning it against an old headstone, she piled snow around its severed trunk. Satisfied that it would live until the following Christmas, she left for home. The next day when she returned, the tree had fallen and was hidden beneath new-fallen snow. Again, she pulled it to a standing position, but each time she visited it she could clearly see that needle by needle, it was dying. Her tree, like her mother, was dead and nothing could save it. Death was final and that was that.

And now, seven years later, she was once again questioning what she had questioned back then: "Why? Why when I need you most, have you not been there for me?"

Cold and alone, filled with self-pity, she sat in the day's silence. She didn't consider the tremendous burden her father had carried as a widower with six children, one of whom he had recently buried, but chose to think of how much she resented him and her life.

Suddenly a neighbor's cat walked across the snow, leaving small paw prints that looked strangely like miniature footprints. Smiling slightly, Mary tilted her head and thought of how wonderful it would be to live in a warm place near the ocean. The sun would always shine. With closed eyes she imagined the beach, heard the waves as they met with the shore, and heard the seabirds as they dove for their endless supply of food. She could not help but won der why God took care of the birds while leaving her so hungry.

Still lingering in self-pity, she suddenly remembered something quite remarkable about the Christmas tree after it had died. When spring had arrived, out of the hard-packed earth where her tree had stood, a small green pine was growing. It was standing straight, rooted firmly, its tiny virgin branches extended toward the heavens as though inviting an embrace. Something amazing, something marvelous had occurred—beyond explanation. She had thought about if for a long time, but had since forgotten that out of death new life is born.

She remained silent, as if considering something. She looked away, her face disturbed. Placing a chapped hand inside her jacket pocket for warmth she discovered the stub of a pencil and a blank piece of yellow notebook paper she had stuffed there earlier. Slowly she unfolded the paper, and while staring at the cat's footprints in the snow, she imagined that she was walking across sun-bleached sands. Almost as if it had a life of its own, the pencil began to move across the paper.

One night I dreamed I was walking along the beach with the Lord. Many scenes from my life flashed across the sky. In each scene I noticed footprints in the sand. Sometimes there were two sets of footprints. Other times there were one set of footprints. This bothered me because I noticed that during the low periods of my life when I was suffering from anguish, sorrow, or defeat, I could see only one set of footprints, so I said to the Lord, "You promised me, Lord, that if I followed you, you would walk with me always. But I noticed that during the most trying periods of my life there have only been one set of prints in the sand. Why, when I needed you most, you have not been there for me?" The Lord replied, "The times when you have seen only one set of footprints is when I carried you."

Tony's Serenade

"He was awake a long time before he remembered that his heart was broken."
—*Ernest Hemingway*

THE NIGHT WAS COOL and refreshing as Mary walked toward a brick building not far from her home. Even in the city, the air was aromatic with the promised scents of early spring. The voice of the Delaware River mingled with the songs of birds. Her father said now that she was fifteen, she would be permitted to attend the firehouse Saturday night dances, but that was all. "I'll be there, so I expect you to act like a lady," he had earlier warned.

Mary hesitated at the entranceway to the square hall. After letting the music relax her, she finally entered. She was leaning against the hard wall, tensely, when she noticed a young man in the distance. A thick mass of black hair framed a strongly formed face. His nose was faintly aquiline and his dark eyes were so intense that they demanded her attention. He smiled in her direction as he noted her stare.

Instead of feeling embarrassed by her sudden boldness, Mary became mystified by the unexpected current that rocked her body. As he walked toward her she began to feel her skin burn. The strange stirrings were both disturbing and wonderful.

"Would you like to dance?" he asked as he put his hand on her arm and led her toward the dance floor.

For a moment Mary paused. She was confused and uncertain. Why was she feeling so unnerved by this man's presence? As her bewilderment grew, she managed to nod yes. Holding her close in dance, he whispered that his name was Tony Amalfitano.

At first she gave no indication that she had heard him. The tingling increased in her flesh. She did not know that this stranger was looking down at her with amusement until he asked, "Do you have a name?"

Swallowing, she forced herself to speak through a tight throat. "I'm Mary Stevenson. My friends call me Stevie."

Tony regarded her intently as he drew her closer. "You dance marvelously, Stevie," he murmured.

"Thank you," Mary responded with a feeling of helplessness. For a split second she wanted to tell him that she was the "White Cracker" from Third and Market Streets, but somehow she felt that, like her family, Tony would disapprove of her making a "public spectacle" of herself.

The interest they had in each other was cultivated as they continued to meet at future dances. She learned that he was Italian, that he was ten years older than she was, and that he knew her brother Andy. She also learned that he drove a black Plymouth, that he wore an expensive diamond ring, that he had a good-paying job as a welder, and that he lived in a far better neighborhood than her own on Kerlin Street.

Although she was still prohibited from dating, she managed to sneak off with Tony during dances and drive around town in his car. One evening he drew his car to a stop at a local park. Diamondlike stars broke the blackness of the sky and the atmosphere seemed ethereal. "Would you like to take a walk?" he asked.

Mary laughed. "We can't stay long because my father'll look for me at the dance. He's looked before and I've told him that I was in the ladies room."

Holding hands they walked with other couples along paths that intermingled with thickened shrubbery and mountains of trees. When they reached a bench he gently pulled her down beside him. After a moment she felt a strong arm around her shoulder, then fingers moving gently through the back of her hair. She looked around at him.

"I'd like to kiss you," he said.

Turning her head, she moved a few inches away from him and lowered her voice. "I can't, Tony."

"Are you afraid?"

"No . . . yes."

Rather than being annoyed, Tony appeared to respect her obvious innocence. "Your father's pretty strict with you, right?"

"That's part of it," she replied hesitantly, all the while thinking how warm and caring Tony seemed compared to her father and how, unlike her father, he appeared to understand all the things she was unable to say. Tony was puzzled.

Mary blushed, but she continued: "My brother told me that you already have a girlfriend, Tony—someone you've been dating for a long time. Is this true?"

Slightly pained, Tony shook his head. "Yes and no. She's an Italian-Catholic who's my age. My mother picked her out for me, but she's really not my type."

"What is your type?"

Tony's eyes flashed with humor. "A blond beauty with eyes that change from blue to hazel, a princess who dances like a butterfly."

After a long silence, Mary said, "You'd better take me back to the dance. My father'll be looking for me."

"Will you see me again?"

Mary stared silently into the darkness. The very thought of not seeing him again made her afraid. Turning to look into his eyes, and without knowing exactly where her strength came from, she said, "I don't know if I can see you anymore, Tony. It doesn't seem right to date someone who already has a wife picked out for him."

Mary turned sixteen and with it a certain maturity set in. She continued to dance with Tony and others at the firehouse dances, but, despite her pain, she obstinately refused to leave with him. Many months of misery passed, but she had to maintain her position. Finally, Tony walked over to her briskly and took her by the arm. She looked up at him sharply.

"I need to talk to you."

"I don't like your tone," she retorted as she pulled away from him.

Tony's eyes were simmering. "I'm sorry, but I can't stand seeing you dancing with other guys. I need to ask you something."

Mary tilted her head. "Ask."

Tony appeared disturbed by her impersonal response, which, even to her, sounded harsh. His eyes filled with sadness and dejection as he shook his head. "Stevie . . . "

Mary's eyes moved over his face restlessly. At that moment he was not a man of confidence, but a man who was worried. Realizing that a battle had been won, her heart laughed with secret delight.

Tony flushed. "I can't ask you here. Please, let's go someplace where we'll have privacy." He led her out of the building to his car.

They drove toward the waterfront, and Mary found herself enjoying this rather unbalanced situation. For a few moments they watched a cargo ship go down the river. Finally, Tony turned toward her.

"Stevie," he said lowly, "you must know how much I care for you."

Mary stared straight ahead. "No, I don't."

"You're so pretty."

His compliment made her blush. Trying to camouflage her happiness she continued to look out over the water. She didn't know exactly how to respond. All of a sudden the image of her mother filled her mind and a deep sadness overcame her. She needed so badly to talk to her, to ask her the kind of questions a daughter could never ask a father. Turning, she studied Tony with deep concentration.

Gently, he drew her close to him. "I want you to marry me," he whispered. "I love you."

Mary stared at him helplessly. "What?" she squeaked in a voice that didn't sound like hers.

"By getting married we won't have to sneak around behind your father's back. Marrying will also get my mother off my back. Plus, with your father away so often you need someone to take care of you."

Memories of going hungry and of sitting in the snow and cold made her shudder. She could hear her father's voice as he yelled at her: "I don't believe any of your excuses. You constantly disobey me! The fact that you quit school is stupid! You'll never amount to anything, never do anything worth talking about! Dancing and writing those damn-fool poems will get you nowhere—nowhere!" he had stressed angrily, over and over and over again.

"You'll love my mother, Stevie. And she'll love you. She loves to cook, and you certainly need some fattening up."

As she leaned into Tony, she could hear the sounds of his promises resonating from his chest, promises that sounded like dreams. Although he came from a large Italian family, his family was not poor. He lived in a nice house on a nice street. Images of large, fun-filled Italian family dinners filled her mind. She could actually smell the aroma of pasta, sweet sausage, and homemade garlic bread baking in a warm oven. All the Italian families that she had ever known were warm and welcoming.

Pulling away slightly, she asked, "What about my father? He'll never let me marry you. I'm only sixteen."

"We'll elope. Let's go to Maryland."

"But what about your family? Won't they be angry that you didn't marry in the Catholic Church?"

Tony lowered his eyes momentarily, and for a split second Mary felt a sense of discomfort. But, like a starved child suddenly presented with a life-saving feast, she put all discomfort aside as Tony explained, "None of that's important. This is my life—our life— my mother'll get over my eloping. She'll have to."

The tension of what they were about to do increased, especially when Tony insisted they elope immediately. "We love each other, Stevie. Why should we wait? What benefit is there in waiting?"

Within hours they were man and wife. Mary was so frightened that she barely remembered the civil ceremony. Afterwards, she told Tony, "Before we drive to Atlantic City for our honeymoon, I have to return home and tell my father that we got married."

"Can't you send him a telegram?" Tony suggested, irritation coloring his voice.

"No. I have to tell him face-to-face. Besides, I need to get my things."

Tony smiled sadly. "Okay, Stevie. If that's what you want."

Mary asked Tony to stand outside on the porch while she went inside to break the news. All the words that she had practiced fell to the side. She simply told her father that she had eloped with Tony Amalfitano. To her surprise, her father was so shocked by the news that big tears rolled down his cheeks. "Stevie, why?" was all he could say.

"I don't know," she answered honestly, realizing for the first time that she had not fully thought out this impulsive act. She also realized that, although she was very much in love with Tony, in truth she barely knew him.

"You're too young for marriage," her father continued. "If you were only married a few hours ago, then the marriage has not been consummated—correct?"

"Consummated?" she asked.

"You've not shared a bed with your husband," he explained.

"No . . ."

"Then the marriage can be annulled."

Filled with confusion and remorse, she went over to her father and hugged him tightly, and although she was a married woman, she was at the same time a terrified little girl who wanted her father's approval. "Please don't cry, Daddy. I'll stay home with you until I'm eighteen, and then I'll go and live with my husband."

Standing solid, he stared at her. She had no way of knowing what he was thinking. Turning his back on her, he walked out of the room, glanced around, and coldly stated, "What's the use, Stevie? You've always had to learn things the hard way. What I say or think doesn't count. You've made your bed—go lie in it."

As a flood of tears cascaded down her face, she rushed back outside. Rather than offering sympathy, Tony seemed irritated as he led her toward his car. She didn't want to disappoint her husband nor did she want him to think of her as a baby, but she could not stop crying. By the time they arrived in Atlantic City her stomach was in a hard knot and her head pounded.

"You're still upset, aren't you?" Tony asked after they had settled in a rented room."

Mary nodded yes.

"Then let's talk awhile."

They talked about the ceremony, the beach, the wallpaper on the wall. When all pretense at conversation had faded, Tony suggested that they undress and go to bed. After placing his wallet and some money on a bureau, he began removing his shirt.

"You mean that you're sleeping in here—with me?" she asked incredulously.

He came over and kissed her on the neck. "Honey, you're my wife now. And I love you. Husbands and wives sleep together. You know that."

Of course she knew that husband and wives slept together, but the fantasies of her private world did not match the world she now found herself in. "I'm nervous, Tony."

"That's only natural, Stevie. I'll tell you what. Since this is our wedding night, I'll go out and buy some champagne. It'll help you relax."

As soon as he left the room, Mary locked the door, grabbed her purse and some money from the dresser and ran to an open window where she had spotted a fire escape. It was close to midnight which made the six-story climb down to the street frightening, but she had to get away!

Once on the street she turned and ran toward the ocean. Taking off her shoes, she walked in the direction of lights. The sand had a night wetness to it and the air was misty and cold.

Looking down, she noticed her footprints in the sand, footprints that appeared so alone, so singularly alone. It reminded her of how she had felt when she saw the cat's paw prints in the snow, how alone she was when she had written "Footprints." She had written it with the warmth of the sea and sand in mind, but this sand was cold, and once again she felt frightened and abandoned.

Would her life always parallel her poem?

The words, "The years when you have seen only one set of footprints is when I carried you," reminded her that no one is ever alone. She began running toward the lights of Atlantic City, stopping only to ask directions to the bus depot. When she arrived she was relieved to learn there was a bus leaving for the Philadelphia-Chester area within ten minutes.

During the ride back she kept staring at the beautiful wedding ring Tony had given her: orange blossoms with a diamond in the middle of each flower, three across. Obviously he had planned this elopement before he had asked her to marry him, which meant he knew she would say yes. Bringing the ring to her mouth she kissed it and asked, "What am I doing? Why did I get married? Do I love Tony? If I do, why can't I sleep with him? I've really played with matches this time."

This was not a simple case of disobedience, of skipping school or sneaking away from a dance. "I've married a man I barely know!" she realized.

Day was breaking by the time she arrived in Chester. After unlocking the front door with her key, she tiptoed quietly past her father's bedroom and into the room she shared with Dottie. Without undressing, she crawled beneath the covers, exhausted. The entire night seemed unreal, like a dream gone all wrong. Soon she would awaken and everything would be back to normal. She would get up and make her sister's breakfast, clean the house, plan for the next dance.

When her father peeked in before leaving for work, he did not seem surprised to see her. "Where's Tony?" he asked quietly.

Covering her eyes, she answered him clearly. "He's still on our honeymoon in Atlantic City. He wanted me to sleep with him so I ran away."

Her father's voice did not seem upset when he said, "I see." Pausing, he stared at her for a few more moments. "You get some rest, Stevie. I have to go to work. We'll talk about this later."

Rising, she stood by the window and watched her father leave for work. She began to cry softly. She had wanted her father to hold and comfort her, to say, "Stevie, you're safe now. Everything'll be fine."

That never happened. Even when he returned from work and she had dinner prepared, he said nothing. It was as if the elopement had never occurred, that she had simply gone to Atlantic City under the guise of an impromptu adventure. She actually thought that the least her father would do was ground her for a week. But there was no punishment. Instead, the quiet between them was impossible to pierce; no matter how downtrodden she appeared, she saw no hint of understanding or compassion in his face. An invisible wall had been erected, a wall that left her an outsider in her father's house.

All that was left was the unspoken disapproval that charged the air with pain. The assignment Mary gave herself for the next few days was to serve her father and then leave the room in a manner of purposeful waiting. It was all she could do not to look him straight in the eyes and scream, "Daddy! Talk to me, recognize me, even if it's to hit me or lock me in the basement. Nothing could be worse than this, nothing!"

Seeking Sanctuary

"Happiness is not being pained in body or troubled in mind."
—*Thomas Jefferson*

BEING IGNORED BY HER father only increased Mary's vulnerability as Tony tried to re-enter her life.

One day he waited for her to leave her house to corner her and beg her to come back to him.

"Stevie," he pleaded, "I'm sorry that I scared you. I keep forgetting how young you are."

He led her toward his car, and she found herself walking willingly.

"Let's give this marriage a chance. At least come home with me to my family's house. Meet them, let them meet you. Please, honey?"

His plea filled her with relief, and like a swimmer who stops struggling against the undertow, she gave in. She could not stand living in her father's house surrounded by yards of silence and despair. She smiled drearily. "I've missed you, Tony. I'm sorry to have caused you so much trouble. Everything happened too quickly."

"I understand," Tony said in a silky voice. "I shouldn't have pushed you so quickly. But what's done is done. My mother's waiting to meet you. Will you come with me?"

Without speaking, Mary nodded and got into the car beside him. They drove toward his mother's house in silence, yet despite being his wife, she felt like an intruder into someone else's life.

Still, as she looked at Tony she realized that she loved him and he loved her. He was, after all, her husband, and if being married meant sleeping together then that was what God wanted.

Tony's brothers and sisters all lived elsewhere, and Mary and Tony were given a room of their own in his parents' house. "We'll find our own place as soon as possible," Tony explained. "In the meantime try to get along with my mother."

"I try," Mary whispered, "but I don't think she likes me. Maybe it's because I'm not Catholic, or maybe because I'm not Italian."

Tony drew her close to him and said with his usual tranquillity. "So become one."

"Become an Italian?"

He laughed. "No, silly. Become a Catholic."

"Becoming a Catholic will make your mother like me?"

"I think so. You don't have to become a practicing Catholic; just being a baptized Catholic seems to be enough to raise my mother's opinion of people. She rates people by the church they belong to and the crosses they wear. Plus, it'll be easier when our children are born to be one religion."

Having children was the farthest thing from Mary's mind. However, if becoming a Catholic would decrease the distance she felt with Tony's mother, she was willing to become one. And although it appeared that Mrs. Amalfitano made piety her profession, becoming a Catholic would not automatically mean that Tony's mother would become unbending and less judgmental. As it now stood, it appeared that Mary had traded one climate of silent disapproval for another, and she hated it.

By the time she became a Catholic she believed she was pregnant. To verify her suspicions, she made an appointment with the doctor, who confirmed that she was two months along. Tony's mother met her at the front door when she returned.

"I hope it's a boy," she said.

Perplexed, Mary asked how she knew.

"I called your doctor. He told me, and then I called Tony at work and told him."

With tears welling up in her eyes, Mary rushed past her mother-in-law and up the stairs. She threw herself on the bed and cried. On the bus ride back from the doctor's she had rehearsed how she would tell Tony that they were going to have a baby. The moment should have belonged to them alone. And now she had been robbed of that moment.

When Tony arrived home she heard him in animated conversation with his mother, but he never came upstairs. Instead he summoned her down for dinner. Once downstairs he acted as casual as if she had gone to the doctor for a head cold. "Tony?" she whispered as she pulled him aside, "aren't you excited?"

"About what?"

"Having a baby."

He shrugged. "Women have babies all the time. My mother had ten."

Constant morning sickness eclipsed Mary's concern about the coldness she felt from Tony and his mother. All Mary wanted to do was throw up and sleep.

"If you keep soda crackers beside your bed, it'll help with the morning sickness," Tony's mother said without affection.

"Thanks," Mary said. "Eating does help. Normally my appetite's small, but pregnancy makes me hungry all the time."

"You're eating too much. And it's costing me."

Mrs. Amalfitano's response was unexpected and it shocked Mary. She winced. "I'll try to eat less," she promised. She also knew that she would rather starve than turn to her own family. Hearing her father say "I told you so" was more than she could bear.

When she complained to Tony, he reminded her that they would be moving into their own apartment soon. "Just keep the peace," he said. "Mom'll come around once the baby's born."

When they finally moved into their own place she felt like a small child at Christmas. Their first home was completely furnished, with one bedroom and a kitchen. They shared a bathroom upstairs with another apartment. She was happy.

"We need dishes, pots and pans," she told Tony. "Then I'll be able to make dinner for you every night. Which reminds me, we'll have to go grocery shopping."

"Tomorrow. I'm too tired tonight."

The next day when Tony came home from work, he carried some personal items from his mother's house.

"We need to go to the grocery store," she reminded him. "There's nothing here to eat, so I couldn't make dinner."

"I already had dinner at Mom's," he replied, his cold voice sounding like his mother's. With Mary's pregnancy—and thus dependency—Tony acted as if he were confidently in control, as if he alone held the reins.

"That's nice, Tony," she replied sarcastically. "But I haven't eaten a thing all day."

His voice grew even harder as he flipped her a coin. "Here's a quarter. Go out and buy yourself a can of soup."

She felt her back stiffen. "How dare you! I'm not a welfare case, I'm your wife!"

When Tony stormed out of the apartment, she knew that her marriage, rather than being a haven from the storm, was the beginning of a hurricane.

Despite her daily cans of soup, she began losing weight at an alarming rate, while Tony gained weight from eating at his mother's each night. One evening, after he had returned from his mother's house, he found Mary in bed moaning and burning up with fever.

"Damn!" he cursed. "I'm working my tail off while you're in bed all day long. You're acting like you're the only woman in the world to ever have a baby!"

He went upstairs to take a bath, then hollered down, "Stevie, if you're not too lazy, bring me up a towel."

Still burning with fever, she pulled herself out of bed. The room began going around and around. Dragging a towel behind her, she crawled to the top of the stairs and pleaded, "Tony, I'm so sick. Couldn't you have come down to get this towel yourself?"

Her head seemed to explode as Tony's fist slammed into her face. She rolled down the steps until she hit her head on a radiator. When she regained consciousness she was back on her bed.

"There's no food in this icebox, nothing," a voice said.

"I don't want her to die here in this apartment, Doctor," a voice that she recognized as her landlady's lamented, then asked, "Shouldn't she be in a hospital?"

"The hospital's full," the doctor said. "I know her father. He'll be here soon."

Where was Tony? Mary wondered.

"Her temperature's over a hundred and three," the doctor added. "Plus she's emaciated. She doesn't have anything in her to fight back with. I don't think she or the baby has a chance."

As a band of lights swept in wide curves through her mind, Mary knew she was dying. Something within was exploding into fragments high above her. She felt disembodied. But rather than being plunged into deep despair, she was filled with peace. Somewhere beyond herself she knew the exact moment that her father picked up her emaciated body and carried her home. She knew that she and her baby were dying. For a split second the merest shadow of the life this child deserved made her think she should fight to live. But that took too much energy; death would be welcome and she gave herself over.

Someone she knew was comforting her, holding her, but every time she turned to see who it was, the image was gone. Fighting consciousness, she pleaded to go back and repeat that experience, an experience that was far more a reality than was life itself. Wherever it was that she visited was warm and pain-free. While there she understood where she was and why she was there, yet when she awakened, her memory was hazy. While there she never asked for explanations because she knew that she was home, knew that she belonged to that golden world of light, warmth, and love.

With every ounce of energy in her, she fought returning to life. However, because the new life within her was fighting to be born, she finally gave in. Suddenly she was whirling through a long tunnel, away from a bright light, back to where she no longer wished to be. She couldn't determine whether the words that she heard came from within or outside of her: "Someday time will be no more. I will wait for you. You are a child of mine. And always remember that when you see only one set of footprints, my child, I am carrying you . . . "

Finally Mary allowed herself to be healed. She took sips of warm broth offered by her sisters. She didn't want to breathe because it hurt too much, but she breathed in spite of the pain.

"Stevie," her sister Muriel explained, "you're going to be well soon. You were suffering from malnutrition, and you were terribly sick."

Agreeing to move forward and to live, she wanted to share with them the truths that she had experienced, but they were beyond articulation. It became simpler to believe that she had hallucinated, and although she had not been aware of the passing of time, she was aware that something powerful had happened.

In her father's house she grew stronger, and with her strength came a determination to never see Tony again, despite his constant pleadings. "Please, Stevie," he begged. "Forgive me. I didn't mean to push you. It was an accident."

"Push me?" she replied from inside a locked door. "You hit me, you deliberately knocked me down the stairs."

"No, believe me, I didn't do it on purpose . . . "

"Go away. I never want to see you again!"

One evening while her father was away, she noted a pain in her lower back, but rather than interfere with her sisters' lives, she said nothing and went to her bedroom. Unable to sleep, she began pacing the room with a strange surge of energy and restlessness. She finally reached for a magazine and settled back on the bed. A dull ache in the base of her spine made it impossible for her to get comfortable so she began pacing again. Then she tried sitting and reading once more. If it had not been so dark outside, she thought, she would like to sweep the front porch. Suddenly, she gasped. A piercing pain began encircling her womb, and shooting low into her pelvic area. Frantically, she shook Dottie awake. "I think the baby's coming!"

Dottie, now fifteen, ran through a long alley in the black of night banging on doors. She located her father at her aunt's house, and everyone came running. The doctor her father finally found had been drinking, but he came nonetheless. A neighbor also ran into the house. Newspapers were piled on the end of the bed and a bucket on the floor.

"Grab your knees close to your chest, bear down," the doctor ordered.

Mary broke out in a sweat and for a moment could not catch her breath. The pains kept coming, pushing down—hurting, stretching, widening, pushing. The pains continued on and on. Would they never end? How could she bear it? She gritted her teeth and held her breath to keep from screaming.

Her breath released as she heard a familiar voice say, "Remember that I am carrying you."

After a series of low moans and deep pushes, it was over. She had a beautiful little boy now to share her world. She lowered her head and whispered, "Thank you, God."

When her new son began to cry, Mary cried too and looked up at her father. He was no longer the stern figure whom she had feared for so long. Instead his face reflected fear and pride.

Mary smiled in spite of her discomfort, and her hands shook slightly. "I'm naming my son after you, Daddy. He'll be called Andrew Edgar."

After the doctor cleaned the baby and wrapped him in a towel, her father gently took little Andrew and began walking back and forth across the room, talking to his new grandson in low tones. He looked down at Mary and smiled. "I'm surprised that you're not naming your son after his father."

A split second of silence passed between them as she recalled the near tragedy of the past few weeks. The shame she felt for having married Tony Amalfitano in the first place had kept Mary from telling her father that Tony had pushed her down the steps. Instead she simply told everyone that she had fallen. When asked about her malnutrition she had covered for Tony by saying that morning sickness made it impossible for her to keep any food down.

Mary looked up at her father. As she now saw it, they were at a new beginning, a place to start over, and honesty was in order. "Andy's father tried to destroy his son, Daddy. You helped give him life."

DIE TO LIVE

"Never does the human soul appear so strong as when it forgoes revenge, and dares forgive an injury."—E.H. Chaplin

IN TRUTH TOO MUCH had happened between Mary and her father to make a fresh start. Mary's father, her sisters and brother, all had their own lives to live, and in going their separate ways, they assumed that Mary, now with a child, could do the same.

Up to this moment in her life, while her family had watched helplessly, rather than taking responsibility for her actions, she had chosen to blame others. But as Mary gazed disbelievingly at her tiny son, it was as if she were suddenly pushed outside into the bright light of midday: the realization of all she had done caught up with her.

She was no longer a child, nor could she claim to be. She now had a child of her own and she had no idea how she would provide for him. She had little education, no money of her own, no home of her own. Not only had she jumped from the frying pan into the fire, but she had jumped so often that her burns were leaving visible scars.

Carrying Andrew out onto the front porch, she noted that the sky was an April blue. Spring had come. It was 1940. Holding her son close to her, she sat on a rusty glider. From an open window of an adjoining house "You Must Have Been a Beautiful Baby" was playing on the radio.

Smiling sadly, she bent and kissed Andrew gently on his forehead. Looking around she thought of all the changes that had occurred since she had been the "White Cracker" dancing on the corner to the music of Duke Ellington. The "Duke" was now a world-acclaimed composer who, as a product of swing music, had created a sophisticated style of rhythm using a jazz sound he called "Jungle Music."

The face of Ethel Waters came into her memory, and with it Mary found herself humming Ethel's monumental hit, "Stormy Weather."

She had danced in the company of heroes during a time when so many Americans were jobless and hungry. While she had looked forward to Saturday night dances at a firehouse, World War II had begun with Germany's invasion of Poland, followed by Britain and France's declaration of war on Germany. Rather than think about the bloodshed on foreign soil, her world had orbited around the latest radio exploits of Dick Tracy or Little Orphan Annie. "Leapin' Lizards" was a pet expression she had employed as a child, an expression that often drove her family crazy. Saturday afternoons had been filled with four and a half hours of cliff-hanging serials featuring Tarzan, Flash Gordon, and Tom Mix, whose "Reach for the sky!" had given her endless hope.

Then there were the full-length pictures starring her heroine, Shirley Temple, whom she effectively imitated. "You remind me of Shirley Temple," Ethel Waters had commented years earlier. "You have that same impish look, but," she had whispered, "I think my little White Cracker dances circles around little Miss Temple."

The common ground on which she had stood with these heroes was fantasy—that wonderful world of make-believe where hard times did not exist, where the world was filled with rich foods and boundless dreams. And when her real world had to be faced, when she had found herself trapped within the cold reality of hunger and deprivation, she had survived by talking to God and allowing His voice to push her pen. The act of writing poems often softened the melodramas surrounding her.

The thought that America might enter the war did not sap Mary's strength as much as remembering how her thoughtless past had brought upon her a hopeless present and an even more hopeless future. Survival meant she had her own war to fight, but she had no idea what weapons to use.

Mary was so immersed in thought that she did not hear Tony's approach. When she saw him standing on the sidewalk in front of her house she stiffened and held the baby more tightly. She stared at him steadily in bitter silence.

His face was gaunt as he lowered his head in shame. Raising his eyes, he asked sadly, "What do we do now, Stevie?"

Her voice was filled with white fire as she said, "Go away! There is no *we*!"

Tony knelt on the bottom step, and pleaded, "Please forgive me, Stevie. When you fell down the stairs, I was petrified. I thought you were dead."

"When you pushed me down the stairs, Tony," she corrected him icily.

With tears in his eyes, he begged, "Just let me say something. I love you. I don't know what really happened. All I know is that I need you and our son. I've found a new apartment for us, a bigger one. It has a living room, a kitchen, bedroom, and a private bath. It's furnished nicely, and it's only a couple of blocks from here, so you can visit your father and sisters. Please, honey, please give me another chance. I swear that everything'll be different."

"I'm afraid of you, Tony."

Tony hesitated. Tears filled his eyes as he stood and walked up the steps toward her. He touched her cheek gently, then reached down to touch his son's face. "I want to be a father to him, Stevie. I want to give him a nice place to live and a decent life. A son needs a father."

Despite her anger, deep dry sobs of anguish and fear rocked her body. Where she wanted to find hope she found despair. Was her despair because of everything that she had done in the past to create this moment? Was it because she had become a costly intruder in her father's house? Or was it because she still loved the father of her son? She had to make a decision, yet she felt no confidence in her ability to do so. All her previous decisions seemed to have brought tremendous damage. She felt crippled, yet she knew the feeling was unrealistically selfish.

Sensing Mary's predicament, Tony moved in: "I'm not really as brutal as you're thinking. Remember all our good times, Stevie. The laughter, the dancing. And forgive me for the bad times, if you can."

Mary's family had their own reasons for urging her to forgive Tony. Her family did not want the burden of a teenager with a new baby. After all, she had been the one to elope at sixteen. For her to believe that she could undo everything by pretending that she was at the starting line again, or could return to life before the baby, was proof of how immature she still was. Baby Andy wasn't a penciled poem that she could erase.

Mary returned to Tony. She believed that God meant for His children to forgive each other, and she also knew that without forgiveness, life could become an endless cycle of resentment and retaliation.

The apartment was comfortable and airy, and to her pleasant surprise, Tony actually seemed to have changed. For a while, their evenings were filled with laughing at their son, listening to music on the radio, even dancing around the room. She enjoyed making the apartment cheerful, enjoyed planning meals. As Tony picked up a small chicken leg and began to chew on it, he complimented her. He actually licked his fingers. "You're a good cook, Stevie."

Mary bent her head over the hot rolls she was taking from the oven. "I did a lot of cooking at home."

He licked his fingers again. "I was wondering if you can make spaghetti and meatballs?"

"Like your mother's?" she asked cautiously.

Tony drew back abruptly. "She's offered to teach you some Italian cooking."

Mary's nature was to be forgiving. Still she was not ready to reenter her mother-in-law's house. She would meet Tony halfway. "I like Italian food, Tony. Why don't you ask your mother to send over some of her recipes and I'll give them a try."

For a few moments the kitchen was filled with an awkward silence. Tony seemed uncommonly flushed and his smile was wide and vacant. "Okay, Stevie. But we can't stay away from my mother forever. She wants to see Andy. After all, she's his grandmother."

Mary could only nod as she placed the rolls in a basket. She timidly agreed that Tony could take Andrew to see his grandmother, but that it would take some time before she could visit.

Tony stood up and said, "I don't need your permission to take my son to see his grandmother, Stevie. What I want is for us to go to my mother's house as a family."

Mary sighed. She understood that it was wrong to make a man choose between his wife and his mother. If their life together as man and wife was going to continue peacefully, she had to let go of all past resentments. Giving in, she said, "I'll go with you. What about this Sunday?"

"After mass?" he asked.

"Mass?"

"My mother's worried about us not attending mass, also about Andy's not being baptized in the Catholic Church."

Little by little, without realizing exactly how it happened, Mary again became the "wife of Tony's mother's son." In order to keep peace, she kept her fears to herself.

One morning the lady next door knocked on her door to say that the ice man was here and did she want any. "Yes," Mary said happily. "It hasn't been easy to keep Andy's milk cold by leaving it in water in the sink."

She paid the ice man ten cents, then he carried the ice in and placed it in the icebox. After Tony arrived home with groceries, Mary made macaroni and cheese, salad, beef patties and coffee. Tony picked at his meal. "Aren't you hungry?' she asked.

At first Tony avoided her question. "I stopped by my mother's on the way home from work. She had spaghetti made. She insisted that I have some." He looked around sheepishly. "I guess it's the Italian in me."

They each knew the significance of their silent exchange of looks, but said nothing. Instead, Mary cleared the table and then sat on the sofa and played with the baby. When Tony heard the sound of water dripping into a pan beneath the icebox, he asked, "What's that?"

"I bought a piece of ice so that the baby's milk would stay cold," she replied casually.

Tony stood and tilted his head. "And how did the ice get inside the icebox?"

"The ice man brought it up, why?"

In a flash, Tony crossed the room and was standing over her. His eyes flashed with anger, as he clenched his fists. "You let another man inside my home while I was working?"

"Was the ice supposed to walk itself up?" she retorted as she laid the baby on the sofa.

Before she could say another word, Tony slapped her face. "Never, ever, back talk me again," he yelled. "And never, ever, let another man inside my home when I'm not here!"

Firecrackers went off in Mary's skull as she stared up at him. "You're not my boss," she finally said as she rubbed the red sting on her cheek.

A sick shadow darkened his eyes. "You are my wife! I'm the one who's putting a roof over your head, food in your belly! From now on when I leave for work the door will remain locked. Is that understood?"

"Stop it," Mary screamed. "You can't keep me locked up like a prisoner."

"Oh can't I?" he yelled as he slapped her again.

"I'll leave you!"

"What's that?" he asked. "You'll leave me? And go where? Your family doesn't want you. They don't have the money to support you or the baby. You're not educated enough to do more than clean toilets or mop floors. You should know that by now. You've never lived this well. And it's all because of me and my hard work."

"I work hard taking care of the house and the baby."

"Big deal." He crossed the room and picked up a pile of note-book papers. "If you work so hard, then how is it you have so much time to write these stupid poems?"

Moving quickly from the sofa, Mary reached for her poems. "Give me those!"

He smiled in triumphant satisfaction. "You want 'em? Then take them," he shouted as he tore her poems into shreds and threw them at her. "Stupid, damn poems. Who the hell do you think you are, Walt Whitman?"

As her poems fell around her like confetti, she cried, "No, I'm not Walt Whitman, I'm Mary Stevenson."

As the weeks passed it became apparent that Tony was looking for any excuse to hit and punish her: if she whimpered like a coward, he hit her; if she fought back, he hit her. It was as if he were constantly punishing her for having left him the first time. Deep inside, she knew what path she must take. Dazedly she pretended to obey him, while she searched for a way out. She was locked in a private world with a madman, and if not for the baby, she would have found a way to escape immediately.

To be sure Mary didn't escape, Tony had a lock put on their

apartment door that could only be unlocked from the outside. It didn't seem to matter that this imprisonment placed their son in danger. Tony began to eat all of his meals at his mother's again. He took care to buy milk for the baby, and when he came home he gave Mary money to run to the store across the street to buy a can of soup. He allowed her seven minutes, and even placed an alarm clock on the window sill to time her. Without looking up, she knew that he was watching her every move, knew also that he knew she would not try to escape as long as the baby was in the apartment with him.

As Mary grew thinner, Tony swelled with satisfaction. But at least her apparent physical weakness lessened the beatings. A thousand times over she asked God, "Why?" Why had she been locked in a cage with a roaring monster? As she thought of what he was doing, a hot, thick rage rose in her throat, but she calmed herself by saying, "Hold on. Andy is growing older—your moment will come."

While Tony was at work and while Andrew slept, the music of her soul poured out onto paper. She remembered "Footprints," and knew that God was again carrying her as she wrote. When this occurred, she was no longer filled with false illusions. Life had not robbed her of her dreams. If anything, her dreams were even loftier now. She was still deeply frightened, but she was also uplifted and her spirit soared. Somehow, soon, she would escape Tony Amalfitano forever.

One morning when he was late for work, Tony forgot to lock the door behind him. As soon as he was out of sight, Mary shoved clothing and bottles into a suitcase, grabbed nine-month-old Andrew, and ran out the door. She had to find her older sister.

"Oh my God!" Helen screamed when she saw Mary. "Tony's been beating and starving you!"

"I've got to get away from here, Helen," she pleaded as Helen prepared her some food.

"Stay here."

"No! Tony'll find me and kill me, I know he will. He's insane."

"Talk to Daddy."

As she hungrily spooned food into her mouth, Mary's voice rose and shook. "I can't ask Daddy to protect me. He has a job, and he's gone most of the time. And I'm too ashamed."

Helen paused. "Then what are you going to do?"

"I want to go to Oklahoma where Mom's sister lives. Tony'll never find me there. I'll get a job. I won't have to look over my shoulder worrying whether while I'm at work Tony'll kidnap Andy."

"He'd do that?"

"He said that if I leave him and take the baby, he and his mother have the money to take me to court and prove me an unfit mother."

Helen hesitated. "I don't like you going so far away."

"It won't be forever," Mary said as she frantically looked around, expecting any moment to find Tony banging on the door. "Can you loan me the money for a train ticket? I'll pay you back as soon as I can."

Once the train pulled into Claremore, Oklahoma, Mary was certain her troubles were over: she was out of reach of Tony's fists.

It was nighttime and it was snowing. Cradling Andrew in one arm and a small suitcase in another, she felt euphoric as Bing Crosby's "White Christmas" played in the background. Her sister had loaned her some extra money for a taxi so she could get to her aunt's house, but when she arrived, the house was totally dark. Perhaps her aunt was out for the evening? After paying the driver, she went up to the door and rang the bell. No one answered. She peered into various windows. The house was empty. Panic stricken, Mary crossed the street to a neighboring house clutching Andrew tightly to her. She was told that her aunt had moved to Texas only the day before.

Her face tightened in terror. What should she do? Where could she go? The cab had already left. "Thank you," she said woodenly to the older woman at the door.

As frozen tears ran down her reddened cheeks and onto her baby's blanket, she turned away. It was so late, and it was snowing. She didn't have the money to buy a return ticket home. She wandered aimlessly up one street, down the other. She was hungry again, cold again, and, this time, truly homeless. It was only when she sank to the icy ground and leaned against a tree that she realized she was in a small park. Andrew began to cry. He, too, was hungry and cold. She took off her coat and wrapped it tightly around him. As she fed him his last bottle of milk, new snow fell. She watched in an almost catatonic state as her footprints were covered with the white sparkling powder. In her mind it was white sand.

"There aren't any footprints left in the sand," she whispered before collapsing into a strange sleep.

Had she not slept she would have noted that as the powdery snow cleared, one set of footprints—stronger and deeper than before—remained.

MOCCASINS

"True friendship is like sound health. The value of it is seldom known until it be lost."
—*Charles Caleb Colton*

"SHE'S ONLY A BABY HERSELF."

In her dreams she was warm, and the voices around her were gentle and kind. As she struggled to regain consciousness, she noted that her wet clothes had been exchanged for warm, dry ones, and that she was covered with a multicolored woolen blanket. An alarming mix of emotions made it difficult for her to speak. She examined the faces that hovered above her. When she saw that they were filled with compassion, she relaxed. "My baby . . . ?" Mary managed to murmur.

A heavyset woman wearing Indian clothing looked down at her from under heavy eyelids. Her dark eyes were shrewd with intelligence. "Your son's fine, child," the woman replied as she pushed a strand of yellow hair from Mary's face.

Mary tried to raise up, but fell back in weakness.

"Be silent," the woman urged. "Rest. You've a long way to go to regain strength. Little Eaglefeather is well fed and he sleeps."

"Little Eaglefeather?"

"My name is Ruby Miles. I'm Cheyenne. I call your son Little Eaglefeather because he reminds me of a little feather, so small, so light. I've been calling you Yellow-Haired Woman."

Mary weighed Ruby's explanation as she looked around the small room which was heated by a wood-burning fireplace, its warm glow casting an endless scene of motion and shadows on walls cut from logs. The flame in an old kerosene lamp swayed with the draft coming from a nearby window. Mary's life had tipped sidewise. "Where am I?" she asked.

"On our reservation. Before the sun had risen, we found you in a park, frozen and unconscious. You've slept most of the day." Ruby looked down at Mary for a long moment, then her voice fell. "You almost left this world for the next. Rest. We'll care for you as long as you need us."

There was a remnant of light outside, but as day moved into night, a gray haze dusted the windowpanes. Mary felt helpless and foggy shapes kept forming and shifting in her mind. Nothing seemed real to her. "How did you find me?" Mary finally asked.

Ruby's eyes, set in a wide tanned face, crinkled into smile lines. "We found you by following your footprints."

As she grew stronger, Mary told Ruby about Tony and how her escape had left her stranded in a snowstorm in Oklahoma. Ruby sat saying nothing, merely nodding as she looked straight at Mary. It was a look of the most profound understanding that Mary had ever received. "I don't know how I'll ever repay you for your kindness. My son and I would've starved to death—frozen to death—without you."

"Starvation is something we understand," Ruby answered. "Our people once lived peacefully in Colorado on land that was plentiful. But once gold was found on our land, there was no room for the Cheyenne. We were forced to move to escape starvation, disease, and indiscriminate killings. Then we were confined to Oklahoma. Whatever we had that was valuable was taken from us."

"Sometimes it's so hard to fight back."

Ruby laughed bitterly. "We fought. But you must remember that when America forced the Indian off his land it was considered a great victory. When the Indian fought back it was considered a massacre." Ruby seemed lost for a moment in her sense of injustice.

"Today we have agreed to treat all men alike, give all men the same love. The sight of our past must give us the strength to not darken our future. We must not repeat the broken promises, the betrayals, the lies of those who took what was ours. For in the end, what they took is neither ours nor theirs, and killing in the name of self-defense is still killing. No man who must kill to live, lives joyously."

Ruby reached down and picked up Andrew, who was playing on a rug by their feet. "My Little Eaglefeather," she purred. "My fat body keeps you warm."

"You love children, don't you?" Mary asked quietly.

"Yes, I do. To the Cheyenne, a child preserves the tribe. Babies have always been prized by the Indians, especially boys. All children are welcomed, though." She laughed. "During the months before her child is born, a Cheyenne mother never stares long at any object for fear that her unborn will be marked at birth. And each morning before sunrise, a Cheyenne with child takes a walk; she believes that her baby will grow in the early dawn. It used to be that after a Cheyenne delivered her baby, a midwife would tickle the mother's throat with a feather to make her expel the placenta, which was then tied in a bag and taken away from the camp and hung in a tree."

Mary smiled, leaning back in her chair, relaxing. Mary told Ruby that her mother had been part Cherokee, but because her mother had died when she was only six, she knew little about Indian customs. "Why didn't they simply bury the afterbirth rather than hang the bag in a tree?"

"The Cheyenne believed that to bury it might cause the death of the child." Suddenly, Ruby gave a brief chuckle. "Today we rub a newborn's skin with powder, but not long ago a mother would grease the baby's skin and then powder it with finely ground dried buffalo manure, decayed cottonwood pulp, or dry spores of the puffball fungus."

Mary laughed. "That's one way to ruin a baby's sweet new smell!"

Ruby answered simply, "Smell also protected a baby." Hugging Andrew close to her bosom, Ruby admitted happily that rubbing a baby with buffalo manure was a custom worth getting rid of. "Little Eaglefeather smells like a baby should."

"I love the way you name people," Mary exclaimed.

"It's usually an older relative, a grandparent, who gives the Cheyenne newborn its name. A name becomes a language in itself, filled with magic and meaning. A boy is often named after an animal, some physical attribute, or even the weather—Little Bull, Soaring Hawk, Tall Thunder. A girl's name almost always has the word 'woman' attached to it: Little River Woman, Yellow Haired Woman."

Mary laughed, then said, "I was just remembering what you said about powdering a baby with ground buffalo manure." She laughed again. "There must have been a lot of newborns named Little Stinker."

Mary learned to trust Ruby and her tribe completely, and in her trust, the torture she had experienced began to fade. Finally, it receded into the depths of her mind, leaving only the thought that God had wanted her to dance with the black folks and chant with the Cheyenne. She wrote: "Learn each other's cultures. Learn to understand and care. I myself have lived with them. And Jesus Christ was there."

Though they had little of anything, they freely shared what they had. The Indians were not a materialistic people; their hearts were their collateral.

Under the care of the Cheyenne she learned how to build teepees, which way to put them up against the wind and the sun, and how to make baby shirts, moccasins, belts, and beadwork. Under a diet of corn bread, tea, soups, and other foods from the earth, she grew stronger. Andrew, fat and happy, became a treasure of the tribe. One Indian made him a doll named Snookums. The only gift Mary had to give in return for all their kindness were her poems, poems that were so inscribed into her heart that no one could ever destroy them.

When she gave Ruby a penciled copy of "Footprints," Ruby seemed to take particular interest in it. "You say you wrote this as a young girl?" After much consideration, she said, "I'd like to stitch this on a piece of fabric and hang it on my wall."

After doing so, just about every family in the tribe wanted Mary to handwrite them a copy. In the eyes of her new friends, she was a woman blessed.

Her letters home were infrequent; she didn't want Tony to find out where she was. One day, without realizing it, summer had arrived. Mary awoke to the sound of laughter.

It was hers.

She realized how very happy she was, how safe, how truly she felt that she belonged. She helped the Indians sell their jewelry, rugs, and colorful beaded moccasins. Most of all she learned to smell the rain before it fell, and she could swear that she was able to "listen" to the sunrise as the Indians did. And the Cheyenne people she loved entered her poems, such as:

Have You Walked in My Moccasins?

If you have walked in my moccasins, you would know.
The smell of rain before it rains,
and you'd feel the cold before the snow.
You would walk proud with head held high.
And enjoy the beauty of a summer sky.

Pearl Harbor was still asleep on a quiet Sunday morning when the attack began that would leave 8 battleships, and 3 light cruisers sunk or damaged, 188 planes destroyed, and almost 2500 lives lost. Mary was particularly intrigued by the news story regarding the U.S.S. Oklahoma, which had taken six torpedoes. "I was terribly afraid," wrote Seaman Joseph Hydruska, age twenty-two, in a news article. "We were cutting through with acetylene torches. First we found six naked men waist deep in water. They didn't know how long they had been down there, and they were crying and moaning with pain. Some of them were very badly wounded. We could hear tapping all over the ship, SOS taps, no voices, just those eerie taps from all over. There was nothing we could do for most of them."

Someone had turned on a radio, where the words of President Roosevelt were being repeated: "December 7, 1941—a date which will live in infamy."

Mary heard a cold voice somewhere within her saying, The world we have all known no longer exists.

The war years created an atmosphere of fear and confusion. People everywhere were being drafted, including American blacks and American Indians. Departing trains were loaded with young men and women who pledged their lives to a war they never imagined could happen. Strangely, Mary did not see fear on their faces—but fear usually arises from understanding, not from a lack of it. It was their parents who looked fearful.

In the midst of all this, one day Ruby came toward her and handed her a letter. Their eyes met, and even before Mary opened the letter, she recognized pain in Ruby's look.

For a moment, Mary stared at the envelope in a stupor. She opened it carefully: "Dad is remarrying," wrote her sister, "and Andrew has joined the Marines. Also, I understand that the Navy is drafting Tony. This means you'll be safe. It's such a terrible war, Stevie, and no one knows who'll return. I know that Andrew wants to see you and his nephew before he leaves for Europe. Can't you please come home? The only thing good about the war—if anything good can ever be said about a war—is that there are lots of jobs for women, so you could possibly stay, couldn't you? We all miss you terribly. Enclosed is money for a train ticket for you and little Andy. Daddy will meet you at the station."

No, thought Mary, no! She looked at Andrew, so chubby, walking, talking, living a happy life without the constant struggle of warring parents or desperate need. Andrew walked over to Mary and wrapped his arms around her knees.

How could she leave this place where money meant so little, but where people saw the value in the human side of everything? She felt like one of those wooden carvings that the Cheyenne made as she stared at the money in her hand. She wasn't sure exactly how to define her fear.

Ruby drew her close, as though she knew that Mary's road had made another winding twist. "You have to return, don't you?"

Mary nodded and then went inside where she could cry alone. After a few moments, Ruby followed her. Mary handed her the letter. "I have to see my brother before he goes to war."

"Of course you do," Ruby said gracefully. "He's your brother. Of course you must go home."

"We'll be back to see you," Mary promised. "I owe you so much, love you so much."

Ruby struggled to find her voice, and when she did, it somehow did not sound natural. They stood looking at each other for a long time before Ruby bent down to pick up Andrew. "We love you as well, Yellow-Haired Woman. But you owe us nothing. You've given us so much of yourself in your writings, words that are the footprints of your soul. We'll read your poems often, copy them and give them to others."

Closing her eyes and inclining her head, Mary saw the steps of her life circling the room. "I don't want to go."

"You must. Another turn in the road has opened for you, a road you have to travel—one that may not bring you back to us."

An early darkness mixed with snow was slipping down around her as she walked toward the train. She held Andrew's hand. In the other hand she carried her battered suitcase. She shook her head pensively, looking around one last time. She had asked her Cheyenne friends to remain on the reservation. Then it would not seem like a good-bye. Ironically, Bing Crosby's "White Christmas" was playing in the background as she boarded the train. She had lived happily with her Cheyenne friends for a whole year.

As the conductor reached for her luggage and led her to a seat, she fingered the piece of paper in her coat pocket. It had remained there a long time, crumpled and folded, but she knew its words by heart, would always know its words. Once seated she looked out the window and saw her footprints disappearing in the distance.

DOWN AND OUT

"If you cannot get rid of the family skeleton, you may as well make it dance." —*George Bernard Shaw*

MARY SAW HER OLD neighborhood with new eyes. Many homes had sagging roofs and cracking walls. Some were empty and had broken windows. Faded "For Sale" signs spotted weed-infested lawns.

She felt like a stranger at first, but soon, within the activity of her family, she began to relax and fit in. It was fun to rummage through her stored box of poems. Staring down at one that she had written when she was very little, Mary thought of the small child with the wide blue eyes who had scrawled, "I wish I were a tree."

Thinking of her childhood gave her a feeling of weightlessness, and as she walked back into memories, her face held a look of repose and love.

Finding a handwritten copy of "Footprints," she read the date "1939" just three years after her first draft. Recalling the snowstorm when she had written the poem, she was reminded that she had never been alone. Instead of God having forsaken her, He had joined her in her walk through life—and when she had been unable to walk, He had carried her. He would always be with her. His ability to carry her and others was the strongest force to be found anywhere.

Smiling, she read the poem again and thought of how often she had copied and recopied "Footprints" as gifts for friends. And how often had these friends told her, "'Footprints' is so inspiring. Do you mind if I send copies to those who need it?"

"Of course not," she had always replied.

Carrying the poem in her coat pocket, she walked through the alleyways she had roamed in her youth. After the first flurry of days with her family and friends, her hours now seemed too empty, too dead. Nothing was as it was, and she again faced the dilemma of providing for little Andy. Her world seemed gray and overcast. Even the snow, instead of being white and new, was a crusted gray slush that covered the ground. When her longing to return to Oklahoma made her remember how much she missed life with the Cheyennes, she would try to substitute motion for thought.

One afternoon she and Andy walked to the platform of the rail-road station. It was crowded with uniformed soldiers whom she pointed out to him. She shook her head and shuddered, wondering if she would ever see her brother Andrew again. He had already left for Europe. Her sister Dottie was studying to be a nurse and planned to join the Army. Helen and Muriel were already nurses' aides. Coming home had its own consequences. Since her father was remarrying, she knew that she, too, had to get her life in order, find a job, and make her own way.

Even after her father remarried and moved out of the home they had rented, Mary remained. She found a job in a sandwich shop but her wages barely paid the rent and the woman who cared for Andrew. To economize, she covered the windows with rags to keep the heat in and spent very little money on food for herself. Slowly, cold and deprivation returned as a way of life, and Mary felt very alone.

One winter evening as she sat in the barren house, someone knocked. Tired from standing all day, she reluctantly drug herself to the door. Standing there was Tony Amalfitano. Out of habit she pulled back in fear.

Tony looked unhappy and embarrassed. "You don't have to be afraid of me, Stevie," he said nervously. "I won't hurt you."

She stood in the doorway for a moment, frowning. "Who told you I was back?"

"I heard. Word gets around." He hesitated. "You look very pretty."

Her whole body remained rigid as she stared at him. He was still a handsome man, but there was trickery in his eyes. "What do you want, Tony?"

"I just came to see Andy." He handed her a package. "I bought him some clothes, a snowsuit, . . . some toys."

"Thank you," she said cautiously.

"Can I see him?"

"He's in bed, Tony. If I wake him he might not go back to sleep, and I'm very tired. I have to get up early and go back to work."

Lowering his head, Tony sighed heavily, then leaned toward her. "Let me help you. After all, he's my son, too."

"No, we're doing fine," Mary lied, knowing that Tony's eyes were taking in her too-thin body and pale coloring.

"Could I pick him up tomorrow and take him out to eat? My mother would like to see him. We are Andy's family, Stevie. It's not right that you've kept our son from knowing his father and his father's family. His name *is* Andrew Amalfitano, not Andrew Stevenson."

As her mind searched for Tony's hidden intentions, Mary reminded him that she was no longer the child he had married. "I'm a grown woman, Tony. You might have bullied me once, but never again. If you do anything to harm me, I'll disappear and you'll never see your son again. Is that clear?"

Tony's eyes showed his astonishment, and for a second Mary was surprised by the force of her voice. But she knew she had to speak her mind while she had the courage. The words had been well rehearsed. Tony seemed to have suddenly shrunk in front of her and looked at her in puzzlement. "Stevie, I know that you're a woman. And I know what you're capable of. I was a fool. I'm sorry."

"I thought you were leaving for the war," she said with less rancor.

"That's true, and that's another reason I need to get to know my son, and he needs to get to know me."

Their eyes locked.

"Stevie," he pleaded, "I may not come back."

Whatever else had to be considered, she knew that Tony was right about that. What if he were killed in the war? How would she explain to her son that she had refused them a relationship? With a great deal of reservation, she agreed that he could pick Andrew up at a neighbor's house the following day.

After that, an uneasy truce existed. They were polite with each other, more strangers than husband and wife. Each was wary of the other to the point that Tony treated her with caution and respect, while she took special care not to offend him.

She was not surprised to find that Tony doted on his son and even wondered if his former behavior had been buried beneath a new maturity. Tony, sensing a softening in her, began to suggest that they have dinner, go to the movies, or take Andrew to the park or to the community swimming pool. She usually refused. Her body still bore the scars of his cruelty, and she would never forget how he had tried to starve her, or how he had held her prisoner and their son hostage in their home. She knew that she could never return to him—no matter how generous he was, how much he swore his love for her, how much he had changed.

She would accept nothing from him for herself, and she grew thinner with each passing day. But refusing everything he offered gave her a sense of freedom from the weight of her past with him.

One evening, awaiting Tony's return with Andrew, Mary felt

stabbing pains in her abdomen. There was a sinking sensation, then the room grew fuzzy, and darkened. What was happening?

Before she could reach her bed, her head began reeling and she fell to the floor. When she woke she was in the hospital hooked up to an I.V. An unfamiliar doctor was charting her pulse and shaking his head with concern. "You had an attack of appendicitis. Plus, you've been starving yourself, haven't you?" he asked sternly.

Mutely, she nodded and then explained her plight. "I have a little boy at home. I need to use my money to feed him. Do you know where he is?"

At that moment Tony walked into the hospital room. "He's with me, Stevie. I found you unconscious on the floor. I was the one who got you to the hospital."

After learning that Tony was her husband, the doctor whirled around. "You mean that you knew she was living in an empty house without food and you allowed this?"

Tony's face reddened with anger as he stared at the doctor and then at Mary. With hatred in his eyes, he stormed out of the room. A few days later a letter arrived from Tony's lawyer stating that Anthony Amalfitano was seeking a divorce from Mary Stevenson Amalfitano and that Anthony Amalfitano was seeking custody of their minor son, Andrew Edgar Amalfitano.

Mary was too weak to cry.

By the time she was released from the hospital, Mary had lost her job. She had no money for a lawyer to fight Tony, and used what little she had to move to a ten-dollar-a-week, furnished one-room apartment. While looking for another job, she took in ironing. In order to save money to reclaim her son, she did without food again. By the time the court date arrived she could hardly walk. She weighed less than ninety pounds. Her coloring was ashen and her eyes lifeless, as if she had not slept a moment since Andy had been taken from her. Tony, well-dressed and well-fed, sat beside his mother and his lawyer at a long table. His mother wore an expensive fur coat over a silk dress. They were bristling with energy and confidence.

The sun crept through the blinds of the courtroom, playing patterns of light and shadow on Mary, who sat at a table to the left of Tony and his mother. She tried desperately to maintain her composure, but her hands shook. She watched the judge read some papers. When he raised his head, he stared at her with what appeared to be both compassion and curiosity. When he spoke, his voice was low and even. "Mrs. Amalfitano, I understand that you've recently been in the hospital."

Mary nodded mutely.

"How is your health at the moment?"

"I'm trying very hard to recover."

"Are you presently employed?"

"No, your honor. But I'm looking for a permanent job. I've been taking in ironing."

"What is your current financial situation?"

Mary lowered her eyes and for a few moments could not answer. There was no way she could lie. With trembling intensity she replied, "I have eleven dollars, your honor."

As the judge reconsidered the papers in front of him, Mary's eyes turned toward Tony: "Please don't do this to me," she silently begged. "Please don't take my son. I've tried so hard."

Tony's eyes held cold mockery. She knew that he had planned—even longed—for this moment. Her only hope now was that Tony's military obligation would take him away before he could take Andrew.

"Mrs. Amalfitano," the judge said kindly, "in view of your current health problems, and your inability to provide a stable home for your son, I am temporarily awarding your husband custody of Andrew."

As Mary attempted to twist herself to her feet, she lost her balance and slumped back into her chair.

The judge leaned forward. "Your distress is understandable. Few courts wish to separate a mother from her child. But the court must also consider the child's welfare and safety. When you're on your feet physically and financially, you may petition this court. However, until that time, you may visit your son regularly."

In the first moments of this staggering awakening, Mary wondered what was left for her. She cried out to God in her mind. After all she and Andy had gone through, why this?

Her one-room apartment was cheerless, an empty tomb. Exhausted, Mary tried not to think of what had been stolen from her. At first she felt no pain, and was actually grateful for the numbness, but her agony quickly returned. Andrew's clothes were everywhere. As she held them to her face, hot tears mingled with his special scent. The light-headedness of hunger made her feel very strange. She fell onto the bed and she woke holding Snookums to her breast. Throughout the night she awoke thinking she heard Andrew crying. During the next few days when she heard the sound of children's laughter, she would swing around thinking it was him. Terrified and desperate, she attempted to enlist in the Army but failed the physical. "You're underweight," she was told. "Try again in six months."

Eventually she found a job at an aircraft factory, asking if she could work the eleven to seven shift so she could see Andrew during the day. But every time she went to the Amalfitano's house she was told that Andrew was not there, that he was "out with his father."

Determined to regain her strength, she force-fed herself. When she was strong enough, she waited, hiding until she saw Tony and Andy leaving the house. Then she pounced, grabbing Andrew and holding him close. As Tony tried to pull their son away, Andrew began crying in fright. Dear God, Mary prayed, was this worth it? What could she do so that she could be with her son?

Although she had put on weight, she had not saved enough money to hire a lawyer. She was saving all that she could, but it could never match the money the Amalfitano's had. She had to find a higher paying job, probably outside Chester. It was becoming apparent that she would have to make an investment in herself before she could make an investment in her son's life.

Taking what savings she had, she took the train to Philadelphia and checked into an inexpensive hotel. After application after application was rejected, Mary knew that quitting school in the eighth grade, eloping at sixteen, and having become a young mother had caught up with her all over again.

She was not good at anything.

Totally depressed, she went into a small restaurant for a cup of coffee and a sandwich. As she sat in a booth by the window, something across the street caught her eye. It was a large sign on a building that said: "Dancer Wanted for Chorus Line."

Quickly paying her bill, she ran across the street. The theater was closed, but she heard music coming from inside. Running around back she knocked on a door. An old man answered.

"You need a dancer?" she asked.

He nodded. "We do. But if you're looking for a job, you'll have to audition now. We close in ten minutes, and today's decision day."

Her voice calm and clear, Mary said, "I'm ready."

After being ushered into a large theater, she was told to sit at a bare table and fill out some forms. She wrote that she could dance, play the spoons, and do imitations of various stars. Finally a man sitting at another table called her name. "Go to center stage."

As she walked onto the stage, she noted how the air inside the theater was rank and humid. Fighting down a feeling of nausea, she sucked in her breath, wondering suddenly, "What am I doing here?"

"What's your song?" the piano player asked irritably.

"What?" she responded.

"Your song, girlie. What song do you wanta dance to?"

"Oh!" Mary's brain did double time. She pictured Andrew's face, saw his outstretched arms. She thought of her mother, thought of Nelson, remembered Ruby. "Do you know 'Sweet Georgia Brown?'" she asked, as she tried to peer beyond the blinding stage lights.

As he began to play, Mary froze. One of the men in the darkened theater rose to leave and she prayed, "I've got to dance. Please, dear Lord, be with me."

Suddenly, something happened: she was the "White Cracker" and the Duke was playing the piano and Ethel Waters was clapping and urging her on. Unconsciously Mary's still lithe body began to move, slowly at first, but as the music deepened with emotion, she began to dance. It seemed as though her feet alone remembered what she could not and once again, He was carrying her.

Chorus Girl

"Laws are spiderwebs through which the big flies pass and the little ones get caught." —Honor de Balzac

THERE WAS SILENCE IN the theater, followed by a round of applause. Even the piano player stood and bowed.

"Wonderful," one of the men sitting at the table said.

Mary looked around in happy bewilderment; she said nothing, but she felt her heart bursting with relief and hope.

"Be here Saturday night. You get fifty dollars a week."

Mary stood astonished by the sum of money she would be paid for doing something she loved and which came so naturally to her. Walking slowly from the stage, she thanked each of the men, then asked, "Do you know where I can find an apartment? I live in Chester. I'll have to move here."

She quickly signed the contract, relieved that they had not asked whether she was married or had children. She knew that dancing girls were expected to be single. "There's a place across the street where lots of our dancers stay. One-room apartments, but they're clean, safe, not too expensive. Tell the landlady that you're with the Troc. You'll be taken care of." The man gave her the once-over. "You're eighteen aren't you? We don't use anyone who's under age."

Her spirits were high. There was a new spring to her step. For the first time in a long time she found herself grinning. Finally she had a chance to earn a decent living.

The Philadelphia Troc was a burlesque house, and although Mary had never been to such a theater, she learned that most of the great comics had begun their careers in places like the Troc, doing humorous caricatures and comic skits that were fun and harmless. However, she was embarrassed by the off-color jokes, and the skimpy costumes she had to wear made her blush.

But none of this troubled her as much as the reaction of her family when she told them where she was working.

"The Troc is a burlesque house!" her father cried out. "Do you have any idea what kind of women dance there?"

Finding herself on the defensive, she began to summarize succinctly why dancing was the only talent she had that would earn her a decent living. "Plus, I've met the other girls. They're warm and wonderful."

". . . and loose?" he shot back.

Once again, Mary was making a spectacle of herself and putting her family name on the line. Her family's attitude, rather than bringing her down, made her determined to prove them wrong.

"And what if Tony discovers that the mother of his child is dancing at a burlesque house?" her father added. "That'd be all the ammunition he'd need to get permanent custody of Andy!"

"That's something I have to risk," she retaliated. "I doubt Tony even knows that the Troc exists, and I'm using a stage name. Besides, Tony has a war to worry about."

Her voice softened. "And we're not loose women, Daddy." She knew that her family's reaction sprang from their love for her. She also knew that none of them could support her or Andy. She had to make her way in life, and they would have to accept that dancing was the only talent she had.

As she settled into her new apartment in Philadelphia, Mary discovered that she was no longer frozen with fear, nor was she agonizing over the decision she had made. All her life there had been others to tell her what to do and what not to do. She put aside the shame she had felt in the past for not being like the rest of her family and took pride in her rebellion. She walked to a different beat, the beat of music. For her, the only path toward regaining custody of Andy was dancing, at least for the moment. Sustained by the dream of earning and saving enough money to provide a decent life for her son, she made certain that her dancing lacked neither energy nor originality. It wasn't long before the Troc asked her to do humorous caricatures in addition to her chorus dancing. She received loud rounds of applause for her imitations of Ella Fitzgerald, Kay Star, Shirley Temple, and the audience's favorite, Mae West. She was able to imitate star dancers such as Fred Astaire, Bo Jangles, James Cagney, and Gene Kelly. Her jumping rope and dancing routine also drew a loud round of applause.

She loved everything about show business, particularly the big buildup before she made her entrance from behind the curtains. The costumes were beautiful and when she danced she felt as though heaven had opened up. She felt that the joy of dancing and singing came from God—and that God meant for His children to be happy. She could not imagine a world without music, dance, and song, or a God who frowned or who had woven His children out of fabrics that were dull and gray. How dreary!

With three shows a day and rehearsals in between, there was little time for self-pity. Each night after the last show, the cast would go out for coffee and food. Even the headline comics joined in. A bond of friendship was born out of common goals. They were a volatile mix of raw and warm people. Each had his own life story, stories which were happily and painfully shared. However, out of fear, Mary deliberately avoided mentioning her son. And as she had done on the Indian reservation, she gave out her poems as gifts, rewriting each by hand.

"May I handstitch 'Footprints' on a pillow?" one of the girls asked.

"That would be wonderful," Mary said softly.

"Every time I feel sad, I read 'Footprints,' and I know that the Lord is always there for me. How did you come to write this?"

Struggling for a moment to control her emotions, Mary began to speak evenly. "I wrote 'Footprints' in a snowstorm." She laughed. "It really should have been 'Footprints in the Snow,' rather than 'Footprints in the Sand.' I was dreaming of someplace warm and that's the way my vision went. I just responded to the picture in my mind, or rather the voice I heard. God told me what to write."

Week after week Mary used her body to express what she felt. Beyond writing poetry, Mary believed that dancing and singing were the highest tributes she could pay to God. After all, it was God who had given her the talent to sing and dance. It made her angry that the public often saw chorus girls as cheap little hoofers. The truth was that they worked so hard that there was little time to date anyone from the audience, despite the onslaught of flowers and cards.

Every once in a while a group of well-dressed women, many of them resembling her fur-draped mother-in-law, would picket the Troc, declaring all entertainers to be "disciples of the devil." One sign declared that they were "Heathens unworthy of God's love." None of it made Mary feel cheap or unclean. She knew that the Troc's audience was often packed with people from the very neighborhoods these women represented. Stranger still, many of the performers whom the pickets denounced were the same ones who volunteered to go overseas and entertain the troops. These they applauded.

During the few hours they had between rehearsals, Mary and the cast would get together and pack and ship care packages to the troops overseas. Secretly Mary could not help wondering when Tony would be sent overseas. Inside each package they included personal letters of cheer. "When we're truly honest with ourselves,"

Mary confided to a friend, "it's how we live our lives that determines what kind of a person we are. I believe that only by giving do we find life."

In the meantime Mary telephoned Andy daily, although the Amalfitanos frequently refused to let her speak with him. She sent him presents. She was cautious never to admit where she was working or that she was saving her money. If Tony could assault her because she had let the ice man into the house, there was no telling what he might do if he knew she was an entertainer who danced before the eyes of hundreds of men.

Mary understood that Tony's behavior must have been born from circumstances that would always elude her. She prayed that those circumstances, whatever they were, would not be repeated in Andy's case. She also knew that should their son ever do anything that the Amalfitanos disapproved of, Mary would be the scapegoat. She wanted to avoid giving them more ammunition.

She thought of what she had told her friends: "When we're truly honest with ourselves . . ." When she got Andy back she would be honest with him. She was proud of her talent and could hardly wait until his young face could see her larger-than-life picture on the billings, beneath which was written the stage name of "Stevie Richards." As her celebrity status grew, her personal struggles decreased.

One night she was standing backstage waiting for her entrance cue. The stage lights were bright. She looked radiant and was excited about the new costume she was wearing. She was the only dancer proficient at the hula and, because of the bombing of Pearl Harbor and America's affection for Hawaii, she was wearing a new hula outfit. The skirt was made of strands of shimmering gold that swayed when she danced. Her pink, flowered top was set off by a lei of colorful carnations. With her blond hair cascading over bare shoulders and her makeup applied to perfection, she waited breathlessly for the musical Hawaiian chant to begin.

While she smiled, she recalled a poem she had recently written called "Chorus Girl" about a girl who only wanted to dance. The people of the town didn't like her, until a flu epidemic hit the town. The only one in the town unafraid to visit the hundreds who were so ill was the Chorus Girl.

"Break a leg," someone called out for luck. She took a deep breath and closed her eyes tightly, imagining for a moment that she was on a sandy beach in Hawaii. She could sense the cool ocean breeze, hear the gulls, feel the hot sand beneath her feet.

Opening her eyes, she heard the music swell and, on cue, made a dramatic entrance to standing applause. Her hands flowed gracefully as her hips swayed gently. A simulated golden sun was setting behind hand-painted palms while the sounds of ocean and sea birds intermingled with Hawaiian chants. Even though she could not see beyond the first several rows, she knew that the house was full. The music increased its tempo and as it did, she moved center stage and forward, her hips shaking with increasing speed. Suddenly her breath caught and her heart stopped.

Sitting in the front row with unguarded shock on his face was Tony Amalfitano.

RENDEZVOUS WITH GRIEF

"Power does not corrupt men; but fools, if they get into a position of power, corrupt power."
—*George Bernard Shaw*

"AS FAR AS EVER getting Andy back," Tony yelled after the show was over, "forget it! You've sealed your fate!"

Mary felt like a crippled child groping for something to lean on as she tried to explain that there was nothing wrong with being a dancer. She looked into Tony's eyes, but his eyes seemed harder and even more cruel than before. "I am Andy's mother, Tony. You can't keep him forever."

He clenched and unclenched his fists, and would have hit her if they had been alone. He drew close to her, staring at her with revulsion. "You've lost any power that you might have had by being Andy's mother," he declared. "No judge in America would return a child to a mother who dances half-naked in front of drunken men!"

Her voice remained firm as she struggled not to give in to the fear she felt rising in her throat. "And aren't you one of those drunken men, Tony?"

"If you think my being in the audience is equivalent to your dancing at the Troc, then you no doubt think that cleaning a toilet is the same as swimming in it."

Tony and his family allowed no discussion, no excuses. Mary was dancing at a burlesque house. Nothing she said would make them understand. If she hadn't won their love and respect a few years earlier, there was no possible way for her to win their under-

standing now. In their eyes she was the wife who had deserted her
hardworking husband, the wife who had deprived him of his son
by running to Oklahoma. Now she was a selfish harlot living the
fast life, proving once and for all that they were right in their initial opinion of her: she was a nobody going nowhere.

Mary began to recognize that her reputation might never survive her being an entertainer. To continue was to willingly sit at the
bedside of her own maternal demise. Again she turned to God, and
asked for some direction, some sign that would guide her footsteps.

On one of her visits to Chester she learned that Tony had used
the argument that he was a single father raising a child as grounds
to exclude him from serving in the military. He, with his attorney,
effectively pleaded his case. The draft board agreed and gave him a
hardship deferment.

On another visit home, she was met at the door by her father.
The moment she saw his face she knew that something terrible
had happened.

"Your brother has been seriously wounded," he said gravely.
"His platoon was in the Solomon Islands in the Southwest Pacific.
All but five of his unit were killed. He's being sent home."

As her father detailed Andrew's wounds he seemed detached.
Mary sensed that he was remembering her mother's untimely
death and Nelson's. Her brother was the only remaining son. She
reached out for her father's hand, but he turned away. She understood his rebuke and suddenly felt ashamed. While she had been
concentrating on escaping a terrible marriage and reclaiming her
son, her brother was shedding his life blood for his country.
Somehow her personal dilemma seemed insignificant.

She also recalled the needless plight of her Indian friends,
recalled how many of them lived in one-room shacks nailed
together from plank wood and scrap metal. With neither heat nor
electricity, they often lay upon piles of rags, sick and hungry. "The
souls and bodies of our people are constantly dying," Ruby had

told her upon hearing that World War II had begun. "What about the war here? What about the little Indian children who freeze to death? Because our land was stolen from us, our people have no dreams, their hearts are sick with hopelessness. Yet we never wanted to fight. War is the coward's way of avoiding peace. War, no matter how it's justified, is a crime."

At that moment she decided that she must stop being a casualty of the human war raging between Tony and herself, a war that could make a casualty of their son, a war in which, when all the losses were tallied, there would be no victor. To lament over the past was futile.

Once her brother arrived home to live with her father, they all had to accept the fact that Andrew's healing would be a long, painful time. Mary wanted to help, but, unlike her sisters who were trained in nursing, she knew she could not be of much use. Again, she wondered what purpose God had for her in life. Somehow her brother's plight put her life in a new perspective. She realized the consequences of her own actions once again.

When she went back to her dancing, she could hear the music, but felt as though she were dancing to an invisible beat. Sighing, she listened to the rumble of a train rolling by somewhere in the distance and darkness. She could feel the pounding beat of wheels. She must move on. But where and to what? Perhaps she should accept Helen and Muriel's invitation to begin a new life in California where they had relocated in order to work in a hospital. Both were now married and had homes of their own, and both openly invited her into their world. "Once Dottie's out of the Army, we'll ask her to move here, too," they said.

"California's so far away from Pennsylvania. And from Andy," she argued.

"That's why you should come out here. We can get you on as a nurse's aide at the Methodist Hospital, which is a very respectable job."

Mary winced. Spiritually, she knew that she had done nothing immoral by dancing. Intellectually, she realized that judgments were often based on appearances.

"Plus it's so beautiful out here, Stevie," Helen emphasized. "No snow, always warm. Please come."

The thought of warmth helped tip the scales in favor of California, and Helen was right: working in a hospital was very respectable. Having a respectable job increased her chances of getting Andy back. She could be of no use to any of the three Andrews—her father, her brother, her son—by remaining in Pennsylvania. Sadly, she also had to admit that Tony appeared to be a devoted father.

The whistle of the train sounded.

Like her sisters Helen and Muriel, Mary was hired as a nurse's aide immediately. She was trained to take a patient's blood pressure, temperature, and respiration. She learned the proper way to bathe patients, to dress and undress them, to feed them. She wore her white cap and uniform with pride, and had it not been for missing her little Andy so terribly, nearly five years would have passed perfectly.

Despite the fact that her marriage to Tony had been dissolved by divorce, she held no interest in forming another relationship. Work was both fulfilling and tiring. Still, at times, she felt that she was living in another parenthesis of life, as if her existence were little more than a connection between her past and the future.

One night on her way home from work, she was thinking about Andy when her head fell back against the trolley-car seat, and she fell asleep. When the conductor yelled out her stop, she jumped up and ran for the door, knocking a young man out of the door with her. "I'm so sorry," she apologized. "I almost missed my stop."

"I thought I'd been hit by a cannon," he said good-naturedly.

"Are you all right?" Mary asked.

"Except for the powder burns, I'm fine."

The next evening on her ride home from work she vowed to stay awake but fell asleep again, and for the second time knocked down the same young man on her way off the trolley.

"Oh no!" she gasped as she helped him to his feet. "You must think I'm an idiot."

The young man's eyes held a faint hint of humor. He gave a brief, soft chuckle. "I have to admit that you've got a unique way of disembarking. Could you yell 'fire' next time?"

Mary laughed, thinking what a pleasant face he had. "This is really getting embarrassing."

The third day when she got off the trolley, she was pleased to discover that she shared the young man's regular stop. She had never noticed him before the day she knocked him down. Now he was going down the steps in front of her again. "Fire," she said quietly from behind.

He turned and looked back with a note of interest in his dark eyes. "I was kind of getting used to being shot out of a cannon," he said.

Once on the sidewalk, they looked at each other, and in that moment's silence she heard things that she had never heard before. Without knowing why, she smiled at him. "Hello," she greeted with a softness that created the illusion that she had known him for a long time.

"Hello, Florence Nightingale," he said in return.

With Basil Zangare, Mary began living in the present. Rides home on the trolley were filled with comfortable conversation, yet never comfortable enough to lull her into a nap again.

Over casual cups of coffee in a nearby diner, she learned that Basil had recently been discharged from the military and had a good job with the Continental Service Company. In return she told him of her early marriage, of her loneliness for Andy, and of her love for dancing. She even shared the poems she wrote with him.

When he looked up from reading "Footprints," his eyes were full of awe. "Mary, 'Footprints' is wonderful," he said, his voice barely audible. "You should do something with this."

She remained silent as she looked into his eyes, eyes that always seemed to see everything within her. "What do you mean?"

"You should get it published."

Laughing self-consciously, Mary looked at her poem. She thought of the many copies she had handwritten to give as presents, remembered also how unschooled she was. Poets were learned and gifted people. She had only an eighth-grade education. "Writing poems is only a hobby. It helps me deal with life, helps me listen to the voice of God. But I doubt anything I write is worth publishing. I'm only a simple woman with a simple voice."

His eyes told her he understood her thoughts. Reaching over he covered her hand with his. "Jesus was also a simple man with a simple voice."

She sat still for a moment, trying to grasp the significance of a familiar stillness within her. The warmth of Basil's hand spread throughout her body. "Thank you," she whispered, "for reminding me of that."

There was no awkwardness when they first danced together. Closing her eyes, she leaned into Basil's hard body and thought of how clean he smelled. No talk was necessary. It was as if an unspoken understanding had transferred them onto a higher plane. Being together seemed so natural.

"Any idea how many centuries we've been dancing?" he whispered.

"No," she replied, then with a faint hint of a smile asked, "Perhaps when music began?"

"Another Italian?" Helen asked.

Mary looked at her sister in full understanding.

"This time I'm twenty-five. The other time I was sixteen. I have no intention of rushing into anything."

"Does he know about your marriage to Tony? And about Andy?"

"Yes," she replied, her voice low to keep Helen from hearing the pain that was always with her. She stood silently for a moment. She wanted to tell Helen that Basil knew other things about her: her heart, her soul, the words she put down on paper. "You think with your heart, Mary," he had told her. "And when you do, everyone listens."

"Are you in love?" Helen asked.

Mary lowered her head a little, and her body filled with a surge of warmth—an awareness of surrendering to the future. "Yes," she answered firmly. "I'm in love."

She waited until she was twenty-six to marry Basil, but she felt tremendously new and young. Somehow becoming Mrs. Basil Zangare meant that her nightmare of being Mrs. Tony Amalfitano was truly over. "Sometimes I'm so happy," she remarked to Basil, "I forget what I was once. You make me forget Tony, the hunger and the cold of my childhood, even eating plaster and tar."

He smiled and drew her close, and they danced slowly to music coming from the kitchen radio. "Honey, I want to believe that my presence has closed a door on your past life. But I know how much you miss Andy."

The music ended but she held on to Basil. No dance, no writing of poems—nothing—could erase the anguish and despair of a missing son.

"Now that we have a car, why not buy a home of our own? I think it's time that we get that boy of yours back into your life— our lives."

Pulling back, Mary looked up at him. "It won't bother you to raise another man's son?"

"Your son," he corrected quietly. "He's a part of you, Mary. He's a part of your smile, your dancing, your poetry. And he'll be a part of the children we have; thus he'll be a part of me as well."

On her days off, Mary scrubbed the walls and floors of their new house until each room was spic and span. New furniture and hanging lace curtains turned their house into a home and fulfilled a childhood dream. When Andy's room was furnished and everything was in place, her longing grew. She was more determined than ever to make him a part of her new life, and holding that dream close, she deliberately pushed aside the possibility that Andy might not want to leave his father or the life he was now adjusted to. He had to miss her as much as she missed him! She also longed to have a family with Basil, but felt that her body was rebelling against her, as though some new soul knew that this potential mother had to bring to a close the issues surrounding another birth that had taken place years earlier. In her mind Andy was still a casualty of the war between his parents. She could not bring herself to accept that every time her attorney contacted Tony's attorney about rescheduling a custody hearing, Andy's emotional stability could be threatened. Financially secure, she was now prepared to fight her former husband, despite the fact that he was effectively blocking her every move. "However," her attorney advised, "it's only a matter of time. This hearing can't be postponed forever."

Needing more money in order to pay attorney fees, she quit her job at the hospital and went to work for Athern Model Craft, which was also closer to their home. Assembly work was hard; however, with each paycheck she saw Andy's face. Then one afternoon while working on one of the machines, she felt her forehead. "I'm burning hot," she told one of her co-workers.

"Me too," the woman answered. "It must be 104 degrees in this building."

Two dots of fire blurred her eyes, and a few minutes later, her head began to pound so hard that she felt her neck and back muscles stiffen. "I'm feeling terrible," she said quietly. "I think I'd better go home."

"I'll drive you," her co-worker offered. "You do look bad."

She was prepared to recover by putting a cool rag on her forehead and napping on the couch. But once in her house, she found herself growing hotter as the pain and stiffness accelerated. Hesitantly, she called the doctor. She was not prepared to be taken to the hospital in an ambulance, prepared even less for the emotional roller coaster which the pain, fever, and stiffness thrust upon her.

In her delirium, she recalled nurses and doctors coming in and out of her room, but she couldn't recall conversation. She saw Basil's worried eyes above a white mask and gown, but it took her a moment to remember that it couldn't be her husband. Only doctors and nurses wore masks and gowns.

When her doctor arrived, she felt the stark concern in his eyes. He pulled a chair close, took her hand in his, and taking a deep breath, said, "Mary, you have polio."

Accepting God's Plan

"Prayer is not asking. It is a longing of the soul."
—*Mohandas K. Gandhi*

MARY SCREAMED, TWISTING HER body as if to resist the doctor's indictment. His words were too brutal to be true. "No!" she screamed. "Not now, not when I'm so close to getting Andy. Please, Lord, not now."

The doctor seized her shoulders then gently eased her back down in her bed. "We'll take care of you, Mary. Calm yourself, please."

The pain grew as her right arm and left leg appeared to stiffen before her eyes. "What can I expect?" she asked the doctor.

"Polio is a virus that at first exhibits no symptoms" he explained. "It enters the body by way of the mouth, invades the bloodstream and can be carried to the central nervous system where it causes lesions of the gray matter on the spinal cord and brain. If there's involvement of the central nervous system, paralysis occurs," the doctor added honestly.

Mary's face went blank. "Am I going to die?" she asked with a sudden calm.

"I'm not going to lie to you, Mary. Polio can be fatal if the nerve cells in the brain are attacked. However, there's a fifty percent chance that you'll recover without lasting paralysis. Right now, we're in a 'wait and see' pattern. Remaining calm is essential."

Basil and her sisters visited regularly. Because polio was so contagious, they had to wear masks and gowns. "I brought you a book to read," Basil said tenderly one day.

Mary dropped the book. Anything she touched had to be burned. Polio was very contagious. Like the links of a chain connecting her present with her past, chants echoed in her mind: "The Stevensons are diseased . . ."

Alone, she lay helpless in bed. She felt hot, stiff, and imprisoned in a body that might never walk again, let alone dance. To never dance again was to only half-exist. "Why, Lord, would you take from me the only talent that I have?"

As hot tears ran down her fevered face, she decided that being attacked by polio made it clear that time had run out for her. Meeting God was a wonderful thought, but having lived without doing anything memorable saddened her. "Lord," she whispered, "you've carried me so often. But, if I have to live life as a cripple, please carry me home. Please, dear Lord."

She tried to move her head to look around but moving her neck caused so much pain that all she could do was look upward. She was even helpless to wipe away her own tears. Suddenly a stream of piercing sunlight lit the ceiling. As she stared at the light it took on the dimensions of a golden cross and, with its appearance, a gentle breeze flowed into the room and dried the tears from her face.

Before a tranquil peace overcame her, before she felt the heat being lifted from her fevered body, before being carried away into a misty sleep, she whispered, "Thank you, Lord, for carrying me home."

When she woke she knew that she had been healed. Without hesitation she moved her right arm. The pain and the stiffness had disappeared. She moved her left leg; although it did not move as before, it had regained much of its mobility. At that moment she knew that her illness had occurred for a far deeper reason than she had realized. With her right arm moving fluidly she reached for a pen and pencil that lay on the bedside table and began to write another poem. She became aware that the healing miracle that was pulsing freely through her was a sign that she had been focusing on the wrong part of her body: her legs.

God had healed her right arm—and thus her right hand—immediately. Perhaps he had done so in order that she know that dancing was not her only talent, that an even more important talent was to listen and to write.

And as she listened and wrote, she wondered how long Newton had been hit on the head by falling apples before asking: "Why do apples fall?"

The time at home necessary for her left leg to heal afforded her time to write poetry, and as she allowed the words to flow from her onto paper, she found her inner eye focusing on a beam of light that seemed to come from another dimension. Sometimes it appeared like a liquid golden globe that was warm and close and pulsating; other times it faded. But it always left an afterglow. What was it she couldn't focus in, but needed so desperately to see? And why did it seem so familiar? She realized that it had been with her often. Perhaps forever.

She found herself pushing backward into her memory with increasing effort, as if through the effort she would discover something of monumental importance. In the mists of her mind, she sometimes caught a glimpse of His face. He looked upon her with kindness and seemed slightly amused. When she tried to bring His face closer, it again became a beam of light.

One night she was awakened by a warm glow from within. The light seemed so close, so easily within reach. There were no earthly rules to tell her what any of this meant. Allowing her inner self to be whirled closer to the light—to Him—she realized that she had seem Him many years before, had seen Him again during her sickness with polio. Consciously she had forgotten what had transpired, but her soul knew what it was. It was *Him* and He filled all emptiness. As His light fell downward and upward and out in every direction, she felt as if all body weight had dropped from her, as if the light of her soul had joined with His light. Her spiritual being swayed with the shock of a rediscovery, and the world reeled with the knowledge that all life was in His hands, that there was no need to fight or beg or even question.

She opened her eyes. The small dial on the bedside clock showed that it was three in the morning.

Basil turned toward her and sleepily asked, "Honey? Are you okay?"

For a moment she watched the light fade, not trying to explain it, but not disbelieving what she had seen. She waited a moment more and then said quietly, "All of my life I've lamented being cold, hungry, abandoned. Now I know that I was meant to have these experiences. I know what it's like to be black. I know what it's like to be an Indian. I've known homelessness. I know the pain of having lost a mother and a brother. I know the helplessness of giving birth to a child while still a child. I know the fear of being a battered wife. And I know the endless sorrow of having lost a child."

Not totally understanding, Basil responded by saying, "I know, but that's all in the past. There's light at the end of the tunnel."

A slight smile cornered her lips. "Yes. But there's light at the beginning of the tunnel as well. I always thought I was in the valley looking up, but the truth is I was given the chance to tiptoe over to the Land above. He carried me. And while there I was told that I chose these experiences in order to understand earthly pain. The very experiences I cried over are the same experiences that will give me the strength to help others like me."

Basil patted her shoulder. "We'll get Andy for you. Don't worry."

She nodded her head no. "My fight's over. God also gave me the strength of your love. I need to begin helping others: the homeless and the hungry, the battered and abused women and children. I don't know how, but what I do know is that through my own experiences, God gave me the gift of understanding."

He drew her into his arms. "You've always been understanding."

Resting her head on his shoulder, Mary whispered, "There's an Indian saying that to truly understand a man, one must walk a mile in his moccasins."

"And . . . ?"

"And I've not only walked many miles, but I've never walked alone."

Although she gasped when she learned of Basil's accident a few months later, her newfound strength held fast. Basil had been working when a truck rolled down the hill and crushed him against a pile of lumber. He was hospitalized for two weeks, then had to remain in bed at home for months while his back healed. The money they had saved quickly evaporated.

Still, Mary no longer questioned anything. Instead, she took inventory and, despite Basil's distress over her going to work, accepted a job at the TWA cafeteria. The pay was low, but she enjoyed cooking.

One evening a man came in wearing baggy khaki pants and a well-worn hat. He was tall and thin, and with his shabby clothing, appeared hungry and in need. His face was wind-browned, and lines of weariness edged eyes that appeared highly intelligent. He asked for a cup of coffee. As she handed it to him, she looked around to see if her boss were in sight. This poor soul needed food badly. And after all, feeding the hungry and the homeless was part of her calling.

As she began making a salad, the man asked, "Do you like to cook?"

"Yes," she replied. "Do you like to eat?"

He laughed, as though surprised that he could laugh. She turned and smiled at him. "What do you like to eat best?"

"Garlic steak and salad."

"Well, I've got the salad part down, but I haven't been asked to make garlic steak yet."

He looked at her appraisingly. "Next time I come in, I'll ask your boss to let you cook my steak for me. Would that be all right?"

Leaning forward, she said, "Look, let me fix a steak for you right now, okay? It'll be on the house."

A glow lit his eyes. "That would be fine."

Each day that he came in, she found herself talking to him and liking him, although he was careful not to share his hardships with her. She sensed that he was lonely and friendless. Luckily he usually arrived when her boss was away getting supplies, so her "food-letting" went unnoticed. When her hungry stranger reached into his pocket for a dime for coffee, she covered his hand. "You need to save that."

"Thank you," he said.

About the same time that the man stopped coming in, her boss walked over to her and told her that she had been given a significant raise. Guiltily, she thanked him, then said, "I need to pay you for some food that I gave away free. I was going to pay you with or without the raise. There was this hungry man who kept coming in. You know, down on his luck, hungry, very poor, so I fed him."

Her boss shook his head and laughed. "Yeah, I know all about it. That's why the man told me to give you this raise."

Mary shook her head. "What man told you to give me a raise?"

"That poor man that you fed. He owns TWA. His name is Howard Hughes."

Feeding billionaires was not exactly what Mary had in mind in her "care for the poor and the homeless."

Basil never let her forget it.

Months later, after Basil returned to work, the telephone rang. "Your brother's injuries finally caught up with him," her father said sadly. "Can you come home for the funeral?"

Mary looked at a faded picture of Andy on a table near the wall. He looked so handsome in his uniform. She lowered her head and said a prayer for him, and like an answering echo, she heard God say that her brother was being bathed in light and warmth. She would miss him, but she also knew that her faith had deepened and that Andy was being carried to the Land above.

She thought that nothing could shatter her calm until she returned home to her brother's funeral and saw her son. She could not believe how much he had grown. He would be a teenager soon. How she had missed him!

"You look wonderful!" she cried out as she hugged and kissed him. "I've missed you so much."

Andy looked at her with a hurt and puzzled expression. "If you've missed me, why haven't you written?"

"But Andy, I have—often!"

"I don't believe you. I've never gotten your letters."

Mary did not move. She stood looking at him, then beyond him. Tony must have destroyed her letters to her son. How could he have done that? How could he have used their son to get even with her? Her eyes turned cold. But of course he could do that. After all, he had held her son hostage before. She bowed her head in thought. It would probably do her little good to accuse Tony in public. She would do what she could to have Andy visit with her in California. Then she could make certain he knew the truth.

After the judge agreed that Andy could accompany her to California for a visit, everything went according to schedule. Their suitcases were packed and they were ready to leave when, at the last moment, they were stopped by a court appeal made by Tony and his lawyers. Forgetting her oath toward acceptance and understanding, Mary became so hysterical that her father called in the family doctor. In between sobs she tried to explain what was happening. "Andy needs to know me. If I don't take him with me, he'll continue to believe his father's lies, believe that I don't care about him!" And she sobbed all the harder.

Suddenly the doctor reached out and slapped her face. "Stop it, Mary," he ordered. "All you're doing is wasting your strength and risking your beautiful marriage."

"But what about my son? He needs his mother."

"A son always returns to his mother. The day will come when Andy will be able to make his own choices, when your ex-husband and his family's money will make no difference at all. Prepare yourself for that day, but don't do so at the cost of your own life and the life that you've begun with your husband. There are certain events in this world that are meant to be, and no matter how we rant and rave, we can't always direct our lives the way we wish. Allowing yourself to become a hysterical mess will not only defeat your ultimate goal, but will make you vulnerable to sickness and disease."

"My son's growing up so fast. I've already missed most of his childhood."

"That may be so, Mary. But meanwhile you're missing out on your own life as well. Look around you, look at others who are in need, use your ability and your love to help those who need it. Andy will be all right. His coming of age is just around the corner." Reaching out, the doctor touched her face and then said gently, "Instead of fighting the straw man, Mary, fight to make your life count."

Jolted back to reality, Mary nodded. Not getting Andy for a visit was a terrible disappointment but as she sat listening to the voice of her soul, she heard a symphony of hope. She recognized that God had just spoken to her through this doctor. Tilting her head slightly, she looked at the man who had slapped her.

"What are you staring at?" he asked.

Without hesitation, she replied, "I'm staring at your halo."

A Mom Again . . . and Again

"*Every man on the foundation of his own sufferings
and joys, builds for all.*" —*Albert Camus*

SOON MARY AND BASIL were blessed with a son of their own. Before little Basil could even walk, they had purchased a larger home—a three-bedroom ranch house in Buena Park with a fenced yard for both a toddler and a puppy named Pete.

As their son grew fat and healthy, Basil, unlike Tony, encouraged Mary's talents. "You need to get out of the house. Why don't you enroll in acting classes?"

Mary looked at her husband inquiringly. "Are you sure?"

"Absolutely," he replied. "Not only am I sure, but you can count on me to sit on the front row for your first stage performance."

Under the guidance of Josephine Dillon, Clark Gable's first wife, Mary not only learned the skills of stage acting, but learned two important elements of the theater: Always be on time, and know your lines.

Meet Arizona, her first play, played in theaters in Los Angeles and Hollywood. The applause was not only energetic, but filled with respect, proof of how attitudes toward entertainers had changed. But after a while, dancing and acting became so automatic they lacked challenge, so Mary returned to her poetry— always interesting and satisfying.

One afternoon, as she sipped ice tea at the kitchen table, one of her neighbors began leafing through some of the poems Mary had written.

After reading "Footprints," her friend gazed at Mary thoughtfully. "Mary," she complimented, "this is wonderful. I've seen this poem in print several times. Congratulations!"

Stunned by her words, Mary replied, "What're you talking about?"

"'Footprints' being published . . . "

"Published? I've never had it published."

Her neighbor shook her head, amused by Mary's lack of candor. "You must have. I think I read it on a greeting card."

"Are you certain it was the same poem?"

"I think so. It's been a year or so since I saw it. But I know it's the same poem. I read it over several times. 'Footprints' is hard to forget. I was very moved by it. It's something that once you read you always remember."

Mary looked shocked, then laughed. Secretly she knew that her friend was mistaken and had no doubt read something similar to "Footprints." After all, how would a poem that she had written as a child end up in the hands of some card company? And why would any card company want to print something a child had written? After all, you had to be somebody very important to have your words appear on greeting cards that people actually paid money for.

Although being a mother, a homeowner, and a member of both the theater and political community were satisfying to her, Mary soon became restless. She remembered her commitment to help others and began to direct her energies to people in need. When, through the theater, she met Jenny, an unwed, pregnant, teenage girl, she felt certain there was something she should do. Jenny would soon be without a job and was homeless. In desperation, Jenny had asked Mary if she knew of a "doctor who could help her out."

"Are you talking about an illegal abortion?"

Jenny nodded quietly as Mary led her into her house. She set the table and prepared spaghetti and salad.

"Can I help with anything?" Jenny asked.

Mary understood the look on Jenny's face. "Do you like to eat?" Mary asked.

Jenny nodded. "I'm hungry all the time."

Mary laughed at a sudden memory. "You're not Howard Hughes in disguise are you?"

Shaking her head pensively, Jenny responded, "What do you mean?"

"Just a joke." Mary pulled out a chair for Jenny. "Why don't you sit down. We have some time to talk before Basil arrives."

Jenny sat hesitantly.

"Jenny," Mary began, "I don't believe in abortion, but I also know that my moral beliefs aren't enough to feed and house you during your pregnancy. To tell people how to live a moral life, those are words that flow easily, but when the waters grow murky and dangerous, to jump in with a life raft is something else. Do you understand?" Jenny shook her head. Mary smiled at her almost sadly. "I've had a lot of practice jumping into murky and dangerous waters. Just relax, enjoy a good meal, and spend the night here. We have an extra bedroom. After that, I need to talk with Basil."

"I'm not sure I understand . . . "

"I'm not sure that I do either," Mary said huskily.

That night as she lay in bed awaiting sleep, she kept thinking about Jenny, wondering why God had brought the girl into her life. Sensing her dilemma, Basil turned to her and asked, "Honey, is something wrong?"

She paused a long time before telling Basil about Jenny. With her face close to his, she explained, "Basil, I believe life is sacred. I've always believed that way."

"I agree."

"What's bothering me is I don't know if I can preach that and not do something about it, like putting my money where my mouth is."

"So what are you saying?"

"My *telling* Jenny to keep her baby won't give her shelter, food, comfort."

"Aren't there public homes for unwed mothers?"

Sighing, she lifted up on her elbow. "Yes, but Jenny needs that personal touch." She paused as she recalled the abandonment that she had suffered as an abused teenage wife with a baby. "I had no real education, no place to turn. When I found a job dancing there were always those well-dressed women who carried signs and shouted that we were floozies. The truth was most of us never even dated anyone."

Basil, nodding, sleepily comforted her.

"While those women called us sinners, they shouted that they were doing this in the name of the Lord. But they never tried to find out why we had to dance for a living, never offered to help. They just called us names. Not one of them ever took time to walk a mile in our shoes."

"Or moccasins?"

"Yes." She fell back upon her pillow. "I'm not an expert on religion, but my heart tells me that a person's good only when willing to help their neighbor, not just judge him."

"What about some church helping Jenny?"

"Churches are made up of individuals—mostly good people— but sometimes churches simply become a place for wealthy people to gather and show off their new clothes."

"Isn't that sort of harsh?"

"Maybe. But when I see so many homeless people going hungry in the shadows of those big churches, my heart says it's wrong, and I think: Would the churches today open their doors to to a desperate Joseph and pregnant Mary or to a homeless Jesus?"

Basil nodded his understanding, feeling all that she felt, while at the same time understanding the position of the church. "There may be doors closed to Him, Mary, but sometimes churches have to cater to the well-heeled to stay in business."

Leaning into his arms, she felt Basil's quiet strength, his familiar scent comforted her, reminding her that she now had someone physically beside her in her walk through life. She looked up at him. "Finger-pointing or preaching isn't what I want to do. I need to help people myself, not wait for others to do it. That's part of what my faith is about. If God can carry us, then why shouldn't we try to carry the load for others whenever we can?"

"Which means?"

"We have an extra bedroom, and God has been so good to us—"

Without missing a beat, Basil interrupted her, turning his question into the answer: "You want Jenny to live with us, don't you?"

Moving closer to him, she replied. "Yes, but just this once . . ."

"Just this once" quickly turned into "Just one more time."

Mary looked faintly embarrassed every time she asked Basil to take in another desperate soul. As she placed eggs, bacon, and toast on the table, she rehearsed what she would say to him this time. First, she would remind him of Jenny's success.

While Jenny had lived with them, they had helped put her through hairdressing school at night. During the days, Jenny had helped with housework and the care of little Basil—and even practiced her new trade on Mary's hair.

One afternoon, six months after her arrival, while Jenny was studying some of Mary's framed poems that hung on the wall, she looked over at Mary and casually said, "'Footprints in the Sand'? I've read this before. I think I saw it on a card, or on a bookmarker."

Before Mary could question Jenny about her statement, her charge went into labor and later gave birth to a beautiful nine-pound little girl.

"I'm naming her Stevie," Jenny had declared, adding softly, "To think what I came to you wanting to do."

After hairdressing school, Jenny found a good job and was able to afford a place of her own. On moving day Jenny asked, "How can I ever repay you and Basil?"

Mary's eyes sparkled for a moment and she smiled. "Promise me that someday you'll do the same thing for someone else."

As she held her little daughter close, Jenny whispered softly, "You mean that I should pass the torch?"

Reaching over to touch the silky hair on Stevie's tiny head, Mary had replied, "In a way. Or more accurately, share His Light."

It was only after Jenny had moved out that Mary remembered that she had forgotten to ask Jenny about where she had seen "Footprints."

The more Mary and Basil busied their lives by extending help and love to those in need, the more content they became. Mary had time to write an endless number of poems. Some were better than others, but most people seemed to like the distinctive style of "Footprints" best. And as more and more of her friends read it, she heard the same tale: "I've seen this poem in print."

It was baffling, but her life was too busy to dwell on it, or to even investigate it seriously. She was still certain that people were mistaken. She was only Mary Stevenson—"Stevie"—that foolish girl who had quit school in the eighth grade.

Little Basil was growing into a beautiful and independent child, yet whenever Mary looked at him, she was reminded of her first son. She wondered how time might have changed him. Now that Andy was eighteen years old, she wondered if missing out on his growing years might have erected a barrier between them that would be impossible to cross? Would the Lord be able to carry her this time?

Whenever she looked at little Basil's hands she would remember Andy's baby fingers, recalling how she couldn't kiss them enough.

Would Andy remember how she had held him close during a freezing snowstorm in Oklahoma? Or recall riding ponies on an Indian reservation? As image after image filled her mind, she also questioned what kind of pain Andy had suffered because of their long separation. What had he been told when, as a child, he had suddenly found her absent from his world?

There were moments when she wanted so desperately to recapture what could no longer be, that she wished she could sequester herself back into the past while keeping the present intact. Although the outward tears had dried deep inside, her soul still cried. Joy and heartache were strange allies.

One sunny afternoon while cleaning the house, the telephone rang. Hurrying to pick it up so that it would not wake her son from his nap, Mary's greeting was almost terse.

"Hello, Mom," the voice on the other end responded. "This is Andy. I'm at the Los Angeles airport. I've come to see you."

Portrait of Faith

*"Faith must trample under foot all reason, sense,
and understanding." —Martin Luther*

A SON ALWAYS RETURNS to his mother.

Mary remained in a happy daze for weeks following Andy's
unexpected reentry into her life. Still, she couldn't help but wonder
if there was resentment when Andy saw her hold and hug little
Basil. On the surface it appeared that Andy was delighted with his
little half-brother.

As time passed and renewed familiarity eased tensions, Andy
began opening up. "After Dad remarried, I offered to help him
move. He was downstairs and I was upstairs. He had been getting
some papers out of his safe and had left it open. Maybe I shouldn't
have, but I began looking through the papers in the safe. I found
stacks of letters from you, plus evidence that you'd sent money and
other gifts. Dad had told me that you didn't care about your first
family. When I found out that none of it was true, I confronted
him. We had it out and I left."

Mary shook her head sadly. "You're here now, Andy. It doesn't
help to harbor anger or hatred. The best thing for you is to believe
that in his own way your father loves you. After all, he did everything imaginable to keep you, so he must love you very much."

"Maybe," Andy said with anger. "Or maybe he just wanted to
punish you."

Like a starving soul presented with a banquet, Mary took unre-
strained pleasure in indulging Andy. Down deep she knew she was

trying to make up with material things for all she had been unable to do for him in his childhood. Basil, while always giving her free rein, thought her excessive generosity toward Andy could backfire.

"Andy's eighteen, honey, and needs to learn self-reliance. You're magnifying a guilt that you don't deserve. Don't sacrifice reason to a false sense of belief that you deprived Andy."

"I know that I'm spoiling him," Mary said hastily, "but I need to do this—more for myself than for Andy."

Basil's eyes looked straight into hers, and she knew he understood. She also knew that he was right.

"It'll level out, I promise," she said. "It's simply that his world has changed so fast. His father never even allowed him to learn to drive. Now that he has his own job, his own car, and his independence, I'm sure he'll land on his feet. I only want to lend him a hand."

Glancing beyond her and into the living room where Andy sat, Basil smiled and said in a tone of warmth, "Lend him a hand, yes. But be careful that you don't handicap him by making him dependent on you. Don't become his crutch."

Mary continued to give in to whatever Andy wanted, and she stood silent when he brought his girlfriend out to California so that they could marry. Rather than give him advice she knew would not be taken—to wait until he was mature enough and could support a family—she hosted a three-day wedding and presented the couple with generous gifts.

In this new circumstance, she was not able to summon the same strengths she had given to Jenny. All her wisdom was now based on emotions stemming from having been an absent mother. Her rationale was that Andy, now married and motivated to be on his own, would find his own way on the road to maturity. And if he did stumble once in a while and needed her assistance? Well, what was wrong with helping him back on his feet? She did not really want to face the motives that were directing her actions toward Andy.

One day Mary walked into a drugstore to order a refill of Basil's prescriptions. Ever since his accident, the pain in his back had grown more intense. As she passed the greeting card rack, something caught her attention. She turned around and gazed at the cards. She had never purchased cards to send to friends, but rather had written them herself. But today she stopped at the rack.

Then she saw it: "Footprints in the Sand."

Struggling for breath, she reached for the card, opened it, and read:

> *One night a man had a dream. He dreamed he was walking along the beach with the Lord. Across the sky flashed scenes from his life. For each scene, he noticed two sets of Footprints in the Sand; one belonging to him, and the other to the Lord. When the last scene of his life flashed before him, he looked back at the Footprints in the Sand. He noticed that many times along the path of his life there were only one set of footprints. He also noticed that it happened at the very lowest and saddest times in his life. This really bothered him and he questioned the Lord about it. "Lord, you said that once I decided to follow you, you'd walk with me all the way. But I have noticed that during the most troublesome times in my life, there is only one set of footprints. I don't understand why when I needed you most you would leave me." The Lord replied, "My precious child, I love you and I would never leave you. During your times of trial and suffering, when you see only one set of footprints, it was then when I carried you."*

She took a step back and blinked. She had no way of knowing what to think. "I don't understand this," she murmured. "It's almost identical to my 'Footprints.'"

She purchased the card and during her walk home, she stopped every so often to look at the card. By the time she reached home and handed the card to Basil, she almost felt numb.

"Somebody has changed your poem," Basil said as he took inventory of the card. "It's been changed from 'One night I dreamed I was walking along the beach with the Lord' to 'One night a man had a dream. He dreamed he was walking along the beach with the Lord.'"

Staring at the card in pain, she asked, "Does that mean it's not my 'Footprints' anymore?"

Basil lifted himself up to a standing position, slowly straightening out his pained back. He looked into Mary's eyes and saw her attempt to fight back tears—saw also the tremor of her lips. "I don't know if changing 'Footprints' means it's not yours anymore, honey. A leaf is a leaf. It can never become a stone."

The wheels of her mind were spinning faster, almost as if she wanted to gain speed in order to outrun this new discovery. "Read what it says at the bottom of the card."

Basil smiled sadly. "I read it: 'Author Unknown.'"

Did "Footprints" write itself? Mary leaned gently on Basil, and while he held her, memories of herself as a young girl sitting in a snowstorm, hungry and locked out of her home, watching a cat's prints in the snow, made her shudder. She relived that moment she had written, "One night I dreamed I was walking along the beach with the Lord." She recalled when the Lord told her, "During your times of trial and suffering, when you see only one set of footprints, it was then that I carried you."

Neither she nor Basil knew anything about copyrights or about laws of public domain. Lawyers frightened Mary after her only experience with them: her divorce from Tony and losing custody of Andy.

Initially she wrote letters to the card company and told them who she was, but no one responded. "Do you think I should send the card company this copy that I handwrote in 1939?" she asked Basil. "Wouldn't that prove who the author of 'Footprints' is?"

"You can't chance that. They could destroy it or it could get lost in the mail. Then you'd have nothing to prove that you were the original author."

Basil's eyes tried to both console and educate Mary. "Honey, this card company's making money from your poem. It's to their advantage to perpetuate the myth that no one knows who wrote 'Footprints'."

"I guess they can silence me, but at least they haven't silenced the Lord."

"You know, the Crucifixion was supposed to silence the Lord. But it didn't work. Instead the opposite happened. And when you think about it, the opposite has happened with 'Footprints.'"

She stared at him for a moment and then shook her head. "What do you mean?"

"If 'Footprints' had been copyrighted, it wouldn't have reached so many people. Maybe that was part of God's plan when He pushed your pencil instead of some well-known author's."

As she listened to his idea, her eyes glowed as she remembered the treasure God had given her. "Maybe you're right. God freely gave me 'Footprints,' and I gave it freely as well. Something that's freely given can never be stolen."

"Maybe. But I still think we should talk to a lawyer."

The news was about what they expected. She was told that because she had not copyrighted "Footprints," it meant that everyone could lay claim to it. "Written material unprotected by copyright is subject to appropriation by anyone."

"But I was only a child," she explained. "There wasn't money for food let alone money for legal protection."

"That's the law."

She looked at Basil. He was watching her face. She recognized the reflection of her sadness in his eyes. It seemed very unjust. Turning back to the lawyer she asked, "What about denying me authorship? Even if I can never legally lay claim to it, is it fair that 'Footprints' forever remains 'Author Unknown'?"

The attorney sat looking at the Zangares. He knew that Basil had been in and out of work because of his back injury. "You could try to file claims in order to make the authorship known, but doing so could be very expensive. Do you have that kind of money?"

Mary stared at the sky beyond the window. "No," she answered softly. "We don't have that kind of money. And if we did, it could be used for better purposes."

Before leaving the attorney's office, she had an afterthought. "Life is strange sometimes." Pausing, she said as though her statement might make some difference, "I'm a descendant of Robert Louis Stevenson."

The lawyer appeared surprised and baffled. "And . . . ?"

"I don't know. I suddenly thought of something he'd written: 'The cruelest lies are often told in silence.'" She blushed faintly before continuing. "I think that keeping the identity of the author of 'Footprints' silent is a cruel lie." Her voice trailed off as she stared into space. When she turned her eyes back to his face, she wondered why she had suddenly remembered her ancestor's words. She had never recited them to anyone before, yet in doing so she understood a truth that went beyond the surface meaning of those words. She sensed that a part of her soul had been opened up to the world, yet she also realized that same "part" had come from God—so perhaps it wasn't really hers to claim anyway. Her voice grew softer as tears filled her eyes.

"Are you certain there isn't anything I can do about this?" she again asked.

The attorney looked pensive for a moment as he sensed her pain, but he knew what experience told him. "If I were you, I'd forget about this particular poem. I'm sure that you can write other poems as powerful as 'Footprints.' Only this time copyright them."

No, she thought, "Footprints" was a poem impossible to surpass. The message in that poem was life-changing and memorable because it had come from God.

EVEN SMALL THINGS COUNT

"When I am grown to man's estate / I shall be very proud and great, / And tell the other girls and boys / Not to meddle with my toys." —Robert Louis Stevenson

MARY HAD TO REASSURE the young girl who had written "Footprints" in a snowstorm that to grow beyond the need to claim "Footprints" would be evidence that, in the end, she believed and lived the message of her poem.

A choice to fight to reveal the truth about the authorship of "Footprints" could bring her suffering and would sap energy she needed to help others. "Basil," she whispered as she reached over and touched him in the dark, "I'm not going to fight for 'Footprints.' I'm going to let it run its own course." He appeared a little stunned.

"'Footprints' has a life of its own, Basil. It walks at its own pace, and it leaves footprints of its own."

"It seems so unfair," he answered. "You've had to work so hard at menial jobs when in truth you should be earning something from all those people who are earning off of you. 'Footprints' is everywhere, cards, plaques, coffee cups, bookmarkers. You name it. Everyone's making money from it. Except you."

"Money doesn't bring happiness," she reminded him.

"True," he replied with a hint of humor coming into his voice. "People with two million dollars are no happier than those with one million."

Punching him, she laughed.

"To be honest though, people who make money their god might someday find themselves shaking hands with the devil."

For a moment Mary lay drifting in her own private memories. "When I was young I thought that money was the answer to all life's problems. Having money meant never going hungry or being homeless. Having money meant that you could hire the law to protect you. While I was seeking to know God I was also allowing myself to become a servant to money, without realizing what a horrendous master money can be."

Mary suddenly looked very young again to Basil, and very pure. "I don't think that we ever have to worry about money becoming our master. However, a bit more now and then would serve us well."

"We're not young anymore," she said with a spark of defiance. "I realize this every time I babysit Andy's children. And Basil's growing up very quickly. With so many deaths in my family, I've come to realize how final life truly is for all of us. In the end the only treasure we have is the light that we carry in our souls. That treasure can only be built by acts of love."

"You're right."

"We don't need as much as we used to. In the end, the money we have left can't be taken with us anyway."

His heart was gentle as he smiled. "And if we could take it with us, what we'd cart over to the other side could be carried in a teacup!" He laughed. "A very *small* teacup I should add."

"I truly do like helping people," Mary ventured.

"Uh oh!"

"Basil?"

"What've you gotten yourself into this time?"

"The war."

He sat up in shock. "The war in Vietnam?" Frowning, he looked down at her. "You're not thinking of joining the Army again are you?"

Mary laughed at him. "Idiot!"

Dramatically, he wiped invisible sweat from his brow. "I'd feel sorry for the Vietcong if you did. You'd end up putting them all in a chorus line, or making Indian beads for them to wear, or inviting them here for spaghetti."

She pretended to look annoyed. "Actually, you're not too far from the truth. What I'm going to do is to bake chocolate chip cookies for all our troops."

Although she was uneducated as to how America's involvement in Vietnam had originated, by the mid '60s Mary was concerned about what was happening. This worry accelerated when President Johnson announced that American destroyers on patrol in the Gulf of Tonkin had been attacked by North Vietnamese torpedo boats. Almost immediately Congress had hurriedly passed the Gulf of Tonkin resolution, which authorized President Johnson to "take all necessary measures" to protect American forces and "prevent further aggression" in Southeast Asia. And Mary, like many parents, worried about America's sons and daughters. Unless the war continued for many years, Basil was too young to serve. However, Andy, in his twenties, could be called at any time.

There were already around 100,000 troops in Vietnam, and the casualty count was rapidly rising. Every time she turned on the television she pulled back in sadness. Each young boy wore the face of her two sons—sons who might never return home to their mothers.

Once she had made a decision to help, she telephoned three newspapers with the following ad: "Wanted: Girl Scouts, Boy Scouts, any and all groups. Let's bake millions and millions of cookies. Our boys and girls in Vietnam need us. Oven to go round the clock!"

She added her address and telephone number. Then, all she could do was wait and wonder if this dream was practical.

Within a matter of days her dream became a chaotic reality. The telephone never stopped ringing, nor did the troops of men, women, and children who marched through her door. A box company supplied boxes; three dairies supplied milk, butter, and eggs; five markets donated chocolate chips, flour, sugar, and vanilla. The Marines came by twice a week for pickup.

Her kitchen was open twenty-four hours a day. The ovens were going constantly. Basil would help for a while, then roll his eyes and go off to hunt for a quiet place to rest. For Basil, the sun rose and set with Mary. He supported her in whatever she wanted to do, regardless of the inconvenience it caused him. "Do what you need to do," he would say, "and there will be a pot of spaghetti ready for you when you're hungry." Mary's sisters on the other hand continued to raise their eyebrows. They wanted nothing to do with her project. They couldn't understand her need to give so much when she had so little herself. Undaunted, Mary forged ahead and kept the cookies baking.

The end result was millions of cookies being shipped to American troops in Vietnam. Each box bore letters along with the message, "From Buena Park with Love," and Mary usually snuck in copies of "Footprints." She rarely remembered to sign them, and if she did, she usually just put "Mary."

As August led to December, Mary remembered the importance of Christmas. Not only was it the birth of Jesus, but Christmas always seemed to bring out the child in every person. She remembered the Christmas tree that she never had, remembered also that love was a seed.

"We can't send over cut pine trees," she was told.

From the center of this chaos of baking and packing, Mary decided to ship an artificial Christmas tree. At first her group was told that shipping even that would be impossible, but it wasn't long before a seven–foot artificial tree arrived in Da Nang. Basil rolled his eyes again, until a letter arrived from a young serviceman that read: "I was feeling very 'down.' Then I looked outside and standing erect in 115 degree heat was a giant Christmas tree!"

The little girl inside of Mary smiled.

A flood of letters arrived, thanking everyone for the cookies and the notes. Many mentioned how much reading "Footprints" meant. "'Footprints' has been passed around so often that it's tattered and torn, but somehow, it remains readable," one letter said.

Other letters spoke of the dismay American troops felt over the conditions of the Vietnamese children. "Somehow in our quest for peace," one young man wrote, "we've found ourselves in a number of situations where we feel lost and helpless. We don't know how to help those who are really the victims: the children.

"Some of us want to build the children a school, but the Cong have threatened that if we do, they'll blow it up. It's hard to believe that grown men could kill children and babies."

Mary rummaged through her own closets, then immediately sent out a plea for books, clothes, toothpaste, and combs for the children. She had to find volunteers to help her pack the tons of clothing and at least seven thousand schoolbooks that she helped gather. The Marines picked up the packages and sent them overseas.

When this was done, they started the process again.

"No matter what call we put out," Mary related to Basil, "people respond. The mood of optimism and generosity is amazing."

"Maybe so," he admitted with admiration. "But you got the ball rolling."

"I only gave it a gentle push. It's the goodness of the American people who kept the ball in play. Without them the game would have ended."

"Isn't all of this work wearing you down?"

"Not really," Mary said as she took a sip of hot coffee. "No matter how long we work, fatigue somehow bypasses us." She laughed suddenly. "The other day when I returned home after running some errands, I found a group of ladies in the kitchen. One of them looked at me and said, 'Welcome! Grab an apron, and make yourself at home!'"

"It must be that 'Viet-mom look' in your eyes!" Basil laughed.

Mary looked up from her coffee. "That's what the press is calling us: Vietmoms."

By early 1968 America had almost 500,000 troops in Vietnam, and more were being sent. The casualty figures were frightening, and the war had sparked a national debate. American students who protested the war began to find support within the government. Even within the administration, the consensus seemed to be crumbling as to whether America should be involved in Vietnam.

As the war dragged on, Mary questioned the wisdom of America's role in Vietnam and worried about the crumbling patriotism she saw around her. Nevertheless, the baking continued.

After another long day of frenzied baking and packing goods, the telephone rang. "Mary Zangare?" a male voice asked.

"Yes?"

"This is the President of the Junior Chamber of Commerce in Buena Park. You've been awarded the Distinguished Service Award for having spearheaded Vietmoms." She was dumbstruck.

"What?"

"A parade has been planned in your honor."

Mary tried to protest but she couldn't speak. Awe and surprise over what he was outlining struck her mute.

A few days later, after a corsage of red, white, and blue carnations was pinned on her, a limousine took her on a tour of the city, followed by a parade in her honor. Thousands of people cheered. Still in disbelief, she waved shyly. Everything was happening at once. She received a Vietnam pin, was made an honorary member of the Air Force Communications Service, and was named

"Outstanding Woman of the Year" by the Buena Park Junior Chamber of Commerce.

When the American flag was raised in her honor, her eyes filled with tears as she thought of America's loss, sons and daughters. She thought of her brother Andrew and could hear him say, "The only way to win any war is to make certain war never starts."

The press was everywhere, clicking away as she read the letters handed to her, one which said, "May you be spared for many, many years to continue the good work you are doing on behalf of those who desperately need help." It was signed, "Sincerely, Edward G. Robinson."

Another award was presented that read: "Thank you for participating and congratulations on your accomplishments. May you continue to succeed in your endeavors. Roy Disney, Chairman of the Board, Walt Disney Productions."

Letters of appreciation had arrived from the Secretary of Defense in Washington, D.C., the Joint Informational Services Office, and the President of the United States.

Lyndon Johnson's letter to Mary became a treasure. President Johnson said in part, "I am grateful for the undertaking of concerned citizens like you to encourage and remember our men on the fighting front. You can be especially proud of the affectionate title conferred upon you [Viet-Mom] by the fortunate recipients of your letters and packages. I join you in your prayers for the well-being of our servicemen and for a world of peace."

But the letter that meant the most was a thank-you letter from an Army captain in Vietnam which contained a snapshot showing a small Vietnamese boy pulling on a tee shirt that once belonged to her son.

The parade had almost ended when a young serviceman approached her. He was walking with a limp and in his hands he carried a piece of paper.

"Mrs. Zangare?" he asked cautiously.

"Yes . . . ?"

"You won't recognize my name. But I was one of those soldiers who received cookies. I found this poem in the box and I carried it with me in battle. I was afraid, but when I was wounded and wondered if I'd live, I read the words in this poem over and over again. And when I did, I knew that while I carried the poem, the Lord was carrying me."

He unfolded the poem "Footprints" and handed it to her. "I don't know who wrote this, but I want you to have this copy. Because if someone hadn't tucked it inside that box, I don't know if I could've hung on."

She closed her eyes to stop the tears, but they slid slowly out of the corners of her eyes. "Thank you," she managed to say.

"No, thank *you*. If you hadn't started Vietmoms, I wouldn't have read these words." As his eyes misted with tears, he asked, "Would you like me to recite 'Footprints'? I know this poem by heart."

Unable to speak, she nodded.

The young man finished with, "The times when you have seen only one set of footprints is when I carried you."

His recitation complete, he looked at her and said, "I only wish that I knew *who* wrote this."

AND YOU CARRIED ME

IN THE YEARS FOLLOWING Vietmoms, Mary Stevenson Zangare continued to serve others unselfishly. Although often viewed by her family as "a little different," Mary maintains a loving relationship with her sisters. The sons whom she could not help spoiling have both married and have children of their own. All have "created footprints into their own future." More often than she would have liked, their footprints have carried them far away from her. The closeness she would have liked was not always to be, but her arms are always open to them.

Her father passed to the other side in 1974, but because of Basil's poor health and his need for care, Mary was unable to leave California in order to attend her father's funeral. Over the years they had written and talked. Age had softened her father; age had matured Mary. And with the passing of time, father and daughter were able to meet on new ground where love abounded. Whenever he read the poems that she occasionally sent to him, he continued to ask his rather unorthodox daughter: "Where do these come from?"

Mary's works, beyond helping the hungry and the homeless, have included volunteering at Anaheim General Hospital, where she handed out roses from her garden each morning. Tucked around the stem of each flower was a new poem that she had written—as well as "Footprints." Some were signed "Stevie"—others were not.

Wealth and fame were never part of her mission.

She has realized that putting a smile on a senior citizen's face or removing fear from a small child's eyes was a reward far greater than material riches could ever bring.

The lives she has affected are many. And through "Footprints," the lives she has touched are, and will always be, countless.

Mother Teresa writes her. Presidents write her. But the letters she treasures most come from those whose lives she personally touches.

In January of 1980 her beloved Basil died of a heart attack, and although he has tiptoed to the other side, his footprints are on her heart and in her soul.

He waits for her.

Shortly before Basil's death, Mary met a young singer named Kathy Bee who became Mary's surrogate daughter. Side-by-side they worked together in the fight against child abuse. Songs were written, money was raised. And Mary, with her gift with words, came up with the oft-repeated slogan: "Beat a Drum, Not a Child."

Kathy led Mary back into show business where, as a mother, a grandmother, and a Vietmom to thousands of GIs, "Stevie" began to dance again. They performed together at the Sahara Hotel in Las Vegas where Mary dressed up as a bag lady for a comic skit. When "Sweet Georgia Brown" was played, Mary danced to a standing ovation.

Through Kathy Bee's intervention, in December of 1984 the United States of America Register of Copyrights in Washington, D.C., issued Mary Stevenson Zangare the copyright to "Footprints in the Sand." Mary plans to present the President of the United States and the White House the original pencil-written copy written so many years ago by a young girl in a snowstorm.

One of the great joys of her later years has been receiving reports of the life-changing effects her poem has had on others' lives. However, she takes no credit. In the depths of her soul she knows that she, Mary Stevenson, only held the "pencil that God pushed."

Mary, born a little more than twenty years after the turn of the century, is able to view our turn toward another century. As a widow living alone, she still walks among us. She has retained her remarkable ability to focus on the positive. She is vibrant and alive and rarely mentions the trials of her past—she is too busy reaching out to others in the present. She continues to write poems in order to cheer up friends—especially those who are wheelchair-bound. Her poems remind them that one bright, heavenly day, they will walk again. This unusual ability to look at the bright side continues to draw people to her. Because she has always let the Lord carry her, Mary Stevenson's "Footprints" will live forever, and His will be remembered by millions.

COOKIES FOR SOLDIERS — Housewives in the 6400 block of Myra Avenue, Buena Park, are busy baking cookies in their "Operation Viet Nam." Working at table are, left to right, Mary Zangare, Cynthia Lee, Charlyne Gray, Carol Packard, Marlene Huckaby, Irene Snyder, Louise Du Pree and boys Basil Zangare, Jeffrey Gray and Mark Huckaby. U.S. Marine Corps Air Station at El Toro has offered to fly cookies overseas free. Imperial Containers, Inc., Anaheim, is providing free boxes for shipping. Mrs. Zangare said anyone could help by donating ingredients for cookies, bake and wrap cookies. Anyone who is able to help with donations may call JA 7-7937 for pickup.

Newspaper clipping of Mary and a group of volunteers she organized to bake cookies for the soldiers in Vietnam. (circa 1965)

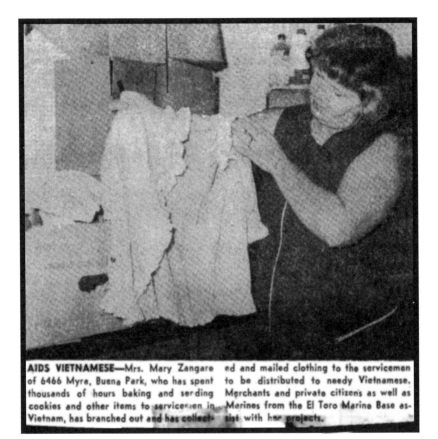

Newspaper clipping of Mary telling of the clothing drive she organized for the Vietnamese children. (circa 1965)

CERTIFICATE OF COPYRIGHT REGISTRATION

FORM TX
UNITED STATES COPYRIGHT OFFICE

This certificate, issued under the seal of the Copyright Office in accordance with the provisions of section 410(a) of title 17, United States Code, attests that copyright registration has been made for the work identified below. The information in this certificate has been made a part of the Copyright Office records.

Donald C Curran

ACTING REGISTER OF COPYRIGHTS
United States of America

OFFICIAL SEAL

REGISTRATION NUMBER

TXU 179-585

TX   (TXU)

EFFECTIVE DATE OF REGISTRATION

December   10   84
Month   Day   Year

DO NOT WRITE ABOVE THIS LINE. IF YOU NEED MORE SPACE, USE CONTINUATION SHEET (FORM TX/CON)

(1) Title

TITLE OF THIS WORK: "Footprints in the Sand"

PREVIOUS OR ALTERNATIVE TITLES:

If a periodical or serial give: Vol...... No...... Issue Date.........

PUBLICATION AS A CONTRIBUTION: (If this work was published as a contribution to a periodical, serial, or collection, give information about the collective work in which the contribution appeared.)
Title of Collective Work: Footprints in the Sand .... Vol...... No...... Date .... Pages. [

(2) Author(s)

IMPORTANT: Under the law, the "author" of a "work made for hire" is generally the employer, not the employee (see instructions). If any part of this work was "made for hire" check "Yes" in the space provided, give the employer (or other person for whom the work was prepared) as "Author" of that part, and leave the space for dates blank.

1
NAME OF AUTHOR: Mary H. Zangare
Was this author's contribution to the work a "work made for hire"? Yes...... No...✓
DATES OF BIRTH AND DEATH:
Born Nov 8,...... Died ......
(Year)   (Year)

AUTHOR'S NATIONALITY OR DOMICILE:
Citizen of ✦ USA .... } or { Domiciled in ....
(Name of Country)   (Name of Country)

WAS THIS AUTHOR'S CONTRIBUTION TO THE WORK:
Anonymous? Yes...... No...
Pseudonymous? Yes...... No...
If the answer to either of these questions is "Yes," see detailed instructions attached.

AUTHOR OF: (Briefly describe nature of this author's contribution)

2
NAME OF AUTHOR:
Was this author's contribution to the work a "work made for hire"? Yes...... No......
DATES OF BIRTH AND DEATH:
Born ...... Died ......
(Year)   (Year)

AUTHOR'S NATIONALITY OR DOMICILE:
Citizen of .... } or { Domiciled in ....
(Name of Country)   (Name of Country)

WAS THIS AUTHOR'S CONTRIBUTION TO THE WORK:
Anonymous? Yes...... No......
Pseudonymous? Yes...... No......
If the answer to either of these questions is "Yes," see detailed instructions attached.

AUTHOR OF: (Briefly describe nature of this author's contribution)

3
NAME OF AUTHOR:
Was this author's contribution to the work a "work made for hire"? Yes...... No...✓
DATES OF BIRTH AND DEATH:
Born ...... Died ......
(Year)   (Year)

AUTHOR'S NATIONALITY OR DOMICILE:
Citizen of .... } or { Domiciled in ....
(Name of Country)   (Name of Country)

WAS THIS AUTHOR'S CONTRIBUTION TO THE WORK:
Anonymous? Yes...... No......
Pseudonymous? Yes...... No......
If the answer to either of these questions is "Yes," see detailed instructions attached.

AUTHOR OF: (Briefly describe nature of this author's contribution)

(3) Creation and Publication

YEAR IN WHICH CREATION OF THIS WORK WAS COMPLETED:
Year Dec 21, 39   1936
(This information must be given in all cases.)

DATE AND NATION OF FIRST PUBLICATION:
Date.........................
(Month)   (Day)   (Year)
Nation.........................
(Name of Country)
(Complete this block ONLY if this work has been published.)

(4) Claimant(s)

NAME(S) AND ADDRESS(ES) OF COPYRIGHT CLAIMANT(S):
Mary H. Zangare
4200 Paradise Rd   # 3063
Las Vegas Nev   89109

TRANSFER: (If the copyright claimant(s) named here in space 4 are different from the author(s) named in space 2, give a brief statement of how the claimant(s) obtained ownership of the copyright.)

* Complete all applicable spaces (numbers 5-11) on the reverse side of this page
* Follow detailed instructions attached   * Sign the form at line 10

DO NOT WRITE HERE
Page 1 of ...of.... pages

Mary's certificate of copyright registration for her "Footprints" poem, granted in 1985.

Mary and singer/song-
writer Kathy Bee.
(circa 1990)

Mary in 1981—back in showbiz as an MC at a dinner club in Buena Park.

Mary in her successful comedy interpretation of a "bag lady" that won her a lot of applause. In 1988 she was named first runner-up in the Ms. Senior Clark County pageant after performing this routine. (Buena Park circa 1988)

Epilogue

THE NEW POEM THAT Mary had written was also surrounded by delicate leaves of gold intermingled with tiny pink roses.

Written fifty years after "Footprints in the Sand," it was its sequel.

And You Carried Me

Oh Lord, you carried me across the sand,
To the mountain top.
You saw every bush and tree,
And every single crop.

When we came down from the mountain,
You said, when you saw my tears,
"My child I didn't want it to be this way,
A world of chaos and fears.

"I gave men the commandments
To let the whole world know
Regardless of race, color, or creed,
I'll always love them so.

"I must go now, my child,
To the land above the sea.
I surely will remember them,
If they'll remember me."

QUESTIONNAIRE

THIS IS A QUESTIONNAIRE to find out how the world-famous poem "Footprints in the Sand" affected you as a reader. If your testimonial is selected it could be used in an upcoming book as well as in a TV documentary.

NAME _____

ADDRESS _____

STATE _____ ZIP CODE _____

Mail your reply to:

> Stevenson Enterprises
> P.O. Box 1417
> Bellflower, CA 90706

Please answer the questions below:
Where, when, and how did you receive a copy of the poem?

_____

_____

_____

_____

Do you still have your original poem? Approximately what date did you receive the poem?

_____

_____

What effect has this poem had on your life?

If, after reading the story behind the writing of "Footprints in the Sand," you would like to hear the music of "Footprints in the Sand" and, for the first time, its sequel, "And You Carried Me," performed by award-winning singer/songwriter Kathy Bee, please use the following order form:

NAME _____

ADDRESS _____

STATE _____ ZIP CODE _____

Make checks payable to:

    Footprints
    c/o P.R. Productions
    P.O. Box 1417
    Bellflower, CA 90707
    Cassette $9.95—CD$14.95/
    Plus $2.95 POSTAGE AND HANDLING

or via:

    MasterCard   or   Visa Credit Card

Expires _____

Signature _____

For additional information regarding Mary Stevenson and/or the author of the book *Footprints in the Sand,* please contact:

    The Arctic Corporation
    P.O. Box 6134
    Gainesville, GA 30504

(Please enclose a self-addressed, stamped envelope.)

ABOUT THE AUTHOR

NEW YORK TIMES BEST-SELLING author Gail Giorgio has written numerous books for such publishers as Simon & Schuster/Pocket Books. Her other titles include *Orion, The Elvis Files, Tuscanini Alley, A Return to the Light,* and *Black Caesar* (now under film option with Lawrence Fishburne). She has written/created and produced scripts, TV/radio commercials, magazine articles, cartoons, videos, audio presentations, and TV shows, one of which was the second highest syndicated show of 1991 ("The Elvis Files" with Bill Bixby.) She is former Vice President of Project Development with Quadra Entertainment Group.

Her works have appeared and/or have been syndicated in such publications as *Atlanta Weekly, Guideposts, Juniors Magazine, Idealist Forum, Globe/Examiner, Woman's Day, Glamour,* and *Atlanta Journal.* She has also authored the weekly newspaper column, "Profiles and Prefaces."

Prior to being a talk-show host with WRNG radio, Gail worked in the missionary field in Oahu with the Hawaii Mission of the Methodist Church. She and her husband, Carmine, are the parents of three grown children and grandparents of five. They live in Gainesville, Georgia, with their dog Chester.

Gail met Mary Stevenson in 1992 and was immediately drawn to her because of her open, caring nature. To Gail it felt part of her destiny to become friends with the author of "Footprints" and be able to write her life story. Mary agreed and the project began. Gail deeply related to Mary's story because of several "connections." She and Mary shared a background of serious abuse, and Mary's

"Footprints" poem had been a help and comfort to Gail when she was going through hard times as a teenager in the '50s. Gail turned down other projects to get Mary's story published because she felt the world should know the true author of "Footprints" and learn from her amazing life story.

Gail Giorgio